How to live
like an
Italian

ANNALISA COPPOLARO-NOWELL

How to live like an Italian

A User's Guide to La Dolce Vita

Foreword by
STEPHEN GUNDLE

PORTICO

To my family: Rob, Francesca, Joe and Tosca, with love

First published in the United Kingdom in 2008 by
Portico Books
10 Southcombe Street
London
W14 0RA

An imprint of Anova Books Company Ltd

ISBN 10: 1 90603 233 5
ISBN 13: 9781906032333

A CIP catalogue record for this book is available from the British Library.

10 9 8 7 6 5 4 3 2 1

Printed and bound by Creative Print and Design Ltd, Wales

This book can be ordered direct from the publisher.
Contact the marketing department, but try your bookshop first.

www.anovabooks.com

Contents

Foreword by Stephen Gundle

Ever since the Grand Tour in the eighteenth and nineteenth centuries, when young men and some women from northern Europe travelled to Italy to complete their education, the peninsula has attracted admiration and curiosity. Like many who followed them, the first tourists were more interested in the past than the present. It was the heritage of ancient Rome, the art of the Renaissance and the natural beauty of the landscape that drew them. Nevertheless, visitors found themselves seduced by the customs and habits of the places they travelled to. Sunshine, blue skies, easy-going social relations, relaxed sexual mores, good wine, and cheap food and lodging all had their appeal. Some travellers took souvenirs of Italy back home with them. The wealthy snapped up art works and commissioned portraits; others, like the foppish *macaroni* in late eighteenth-century London, continued to dress in the flamboyant and colourful manner they had learned in Italy. Many more read the novels and travel books that authors including the French Stendhal and de Lamartine, the English Dickens, George Eliot and George Meredith, and the Americans Henry James, Edith Wharton and F. Marion Crawford set in the peninsula.

Since the nineteenth century, Italy has undergone enormous changes. Unified as a state under the House of

Savoy in 1861, it immediately aspired to take its place among modern nations. While the country's rulers were proud of the artistic heritage, international recognition and economic expansion were their twin aims. However, numerous internal and external obstacles ensured that progress was not straightforward. Italy's political history since the late nineteenth century has not been a particularly happy one. It has known corruption, military defeat, civil war, dictatorship, and system failure. Yet in the decades following World War Two, the country embraced the same values and practices as all the states that were founder members of the European Union. Its democratic system, if not entirely stable, has been in place for six decades and, despite some sharp regional and social differences, the standard of living of Italians today is broadly similar to that of every advanced western country.

Yet the fascination with Italy persists. One of the leading tourist destinations in the world, its historic attractions exercise no less an allure than they did in the past. If anything, the appeal of the Italian way of life has grown in recent decades. Although rapid economic development exacerbated some problems and blighted the landscape, Italy is still widely perceived as a country that is somehow distinctive and different. Compared to Britain, its way of life often seems to be slower and more humane. Time is taken over food and wine, family and community bonds are stronger, there is a more marked sense of belonging to place, and the elderly are shown greater respect. Italians seem to enjoy life and they appear to foreign eyes to have a spontaneity that is enviable. Nowhere is this more evident than in the cultural importance attributed to the body beautiful and to love that was first noted by Stendhal in his books *Rome, Naples and Florence* and *Love*.

Italy offers a humane ideal of life because of the persistence of the provincial dimension of life. The country is not dominated by a single centre and, with the possible exception of Milan, none of its cities could be considered a metropolis. Whereas in Britain, early and protracted industrialisation shattered many local traditions and customs, in Italy much from the pre-industrial era has survived into the present day. The modern and the traditional combine there in innumerable ways. The taste for fast cars, for example, derives from the yearning for modernity and speed that prospered in the backward country of the early twentieth century. The famous Italian sense of style is certainly influenced by the heritage of art and beauty, but it is sustained by a provincial habit of asserting status through competitive display especially by means of the evening promenade. The dominant Italian idea of quality of life – what we know as the *dolce vita* - is inflected with the past. For this reason, many Italian-brand kitchen utensils, motor cars and scooters, and garments that are modern resonate with values that somehow seem to be timeless.

In *How to Live Like An Italian*, Annalisa Coppolaro Nowell draws on her own experiences to present us with a guide to how and why the Italians live as they do. As an Italian who has for many years lived in the UK, she is well-placed to explain the Italian lifestyle and show how aspects of it can be embraced even by those who may never live in the country. Annalisa is from Siena in the heart of Tuscany (sometimes dubbed Chianti-shire) but, as she points out, her father is from Naples. This means that her roots are in the region that the British have elected as the special locus of their Italian dream, while at the same time she has a connection to a deeper Italy that has generated much of the most enduring imagery of the country. Unlike the prosperous central regions, the South of Italy has long been economically disadvantaged, yet almost all the country's best-known film stars hail from there, as do many of its most famous dishes including pizza and pasta. The dark and earthy ideal of feminine beauty that has been symbolised since the 1950s by the actress Sophia Loren is also a specifically southern one.

In her book Annalisa sings the praises of the best things about her native country – a country that, despite all its faults, remains as seductive as ever. With verve and insight, she shows us how we too can share in the Italian art of living well.

Stephen Gundle is the author of several books about Italian history and culture including *Bellissima: Feminine Beauty and the Idea of Italy*. He is Professor of Film and Television Studies at Warwick University.

Introduction

'*The best Italian comes out in moments of difficulty – We turn a crisis into a party.*'

– Beppe Severgnini, speaking at the Italian Cultural Institute about his book La Bella Figura, July 2007

'*Everything you see I owe to spaghetti.*'

– Sophia Loren, who posed for the Pirelli Calendar at seventy-one, in 2006

ITALY, THE CRADLE OF CIVILIZATION.

Italy, where you can find the best arts and food in the world.

Italy, the land of corruption and deception.

Italy, the land of Mafia and Camorra.

How many more stereotypes does it take to describe *Il Bel Paese*? What Dante celebrated in the fourteenth century as *the beautiful country* is today possibly the most loved and equally most misunderstood country in the world.

No western person can call themselves well-travelled if

they haven't been to Italy. And this is not news: great foreign artists, poets and writers have always been inspired by Italy. Culture and learning, science and the arts wouldn't be the same today without Giotto, Leonardo, Galileo and Michelangelo, just like the global fashion industry wouldn't be the same without Armani or Valentino.

Some of the best restaurants in the world are Italian. The language of music is full of Italian words: *forte, piano, sonata, concerto, orchestra.*

And of course *vendetta, mafia, fiasco* and *inferno* are just a few of the Italian words that form part of the kaleidoscopic English language.

Italy features a lot in the news, for good or bad. I am called by the BBC to appear in on-screen interviews to comment on Italian matters on a regular basis. More and more events showcase what we call 'Made in Italy', and our food, arts and crafts, fashion and jewellery are often considered excellent. The Italian Film Festival in London is becoming more important every year and Italian property shows are organised in every corner of the world. Italian language courses abroad are incredibly popular: something that only five years ago was unthinkable.

In the meantime, Italy gets bad press about all sorts of things. You will often hear bad news about Italy, especially scandals, bad politics and services, killings in our stadiums, deaths in the workplace, strikes. They write about Italy having the lowest birth rate in the world, the worst traffic in the towns and a high concentration of trashy TV pro-grammes even on our state television channel, Rai.

So, what is it about Italy? Why are visitors and observers so attracted and yet baffled by we Italians? I have been asking myself this question since I met Rob, my husband-to-be. He was in Tuscany, my region, when I saw him for the first time. He looked lost – something you can hardly manage in a village populated by only sixty people. He was ringing the bell of a house at 2.30 p.m. on a warm afternoon. Nobody, of course, answered. We welcome foreigners, but not at siesta time. But he was persistent, then I appeared in my red 1972 Cinquecento and was able to help him. I helped him so much he became my husband.

This was over fifteen years ago. But the image he has of the Italians still puzzles him. And all of his British family, by the way. Some of them see me as a welcome gift, some of them as a worrying presence, a mine that could explode at any odd time.

I have relatives who are scared of inviting me to dinner together with some of their noble friends, because I'd started talking about pregnancy and birth at a similar dinner 13 years ago. How was I supposed to know that you can't mention the word 'placenta' over celery and stilton soup? We discuss stomach troubles in Italy at all sorts of times. We think there is nothing wrong with 'sharing', we share our beauties and our troubles. So we are slightly unpredictable, to put it mildly.

Books on Italy go from one extreme to the other: in some, everything about Italy and Italians is wonderful, in others, the nation is presented as deeply troubled. The figures published every year in the book *The Top Ten of Everything* are extremely interesting. They illustrate Italy as a country with a lot of contradictions, but also a country where the living is good, despite what you see in the news. We are, after all, one of the eight most powerful countries in the world, but we have the fifth highest level of debt, even if we are fourth on the list for possession of gold. Our life expectancy is the highest in the world after Japan, and Italy is the seventh healthiest country (although we are at fourth place for fat consumption and the fifth greatest importer of champagne). Our economy may be in trouble, but our family businesses are booming, and we appear four times in the Top Ten Oldest Family Business list with wine makers, goldsmiths and even a bell foundry that started in the year 1000. Our fashion industry is growing steadily, our design is still a leader in the industry, and our cuisine is a global cult, second most popular in the world after Chinese, as some American friends who have visited most countries in the world tell me. Impressive figures, but then if you want to find Italy in the list of the countries with most women in politics you have to look at the seventy-ninth place.

Fortunately, numbers aren't everything. Having lived in Tuscany for twenty-seven years, and still travelling there every three months – and of course being Italian – I can say that you won't find the real Italy in these figures. You will find it in the warmth of its people, in the smiles of its children, in the welcoming atmosphere in the squares or in the dances at a May village fête. You will also find it in the thousands of Italian clubs, restaurants and churches all over the world, where our people are respected for their hard work and their unsurpassed honesty and charity towards others. This is because we still have values: it's not necessarily a Christian thing, it's more like an internal gift most of us have that pushes us towards others. We hang on to our family and friends and we try hard to keep our traditions alive, even when we're living abroad. For example, we teach our children to celebrate La Befana on 6 January. La Befana is an old lady who flies around on a broom, bringing gifts to children. The Italian community abroad is usually very visible, such as when London-Italians celebrate La Madonna del Carmine in July: beautiful floats parade the streets of Clerkenwell and there's a huge fair with Italian music and food. It's a major event, in the southern-Italian tradition.

We like keeping in touch with our traditions and with our past, and this, as well as our love for good food and the good life, will be a hard thing to change.

Guido Santevecchi, a *Corriere della Sera* reporter based in London, wrote a very entertaining article about the Italians being the healthiest population in Europe according to a UK university study. He seems to describe quite well the secret of how to live like an Italian: he argues that going home for lunch every day and keeping physical exercise to a minimum works really well for us, just like driving our fast cars on chaotic roads instead of cycling, for example (*Living La Dolce Vita*, the *Guardian*, 4 July 2006). This theory summarises what Italy and the Italians of our times are really like: contradictory people in a contradictory country. But people with a sense of humour, a love for tradition and an eye steadily kept on progress and the future. Although they do have to fight against stereotypes, like most populations in the world.

When I was at secondary school, travelling to Europe for student exchange holidays was often a bad experience at first: the image of *Italiani Mafiosi* was still everywhere in the towns and villages, and abroad they didn't view us well at all. However, after spending a very short while with us the families we were staying with would completely change their opinions of us. I don't deny that, looking at Italy, you do get a lot of mixed signals. Our contradictions are evident, perhaps even perpetuated, in how the rest of the world views Italy and its people. Often, people don't know what to make of us. Some of them hang on to the old stereotypes: warm, loving, friendly, noisy, scheming, charming, feisty, good with children and food, easily upset. Others find the new stereotypes more appealing; the modern Italian abroad is a skilled professional and *'gente bellissima'* with a penchant for the good things in life, for great food and good design, for beauty and parties.

But the largest conundrum of all remains Italy and its 60 million population of cooks, *Mafiosi*, opera singers, mammas, sex symbols, corrupt politicians and good-looking footballers. A land of awful TV shows and good train service, of closed art galleries and magnificent landscapes. What holds this enormously varied population together?

Many have written on Italy and her wonderful secrets, from Tobias Jones to Francesco Da Mosto, but what is missing in some of these books is the perspective on the 'real' Italian, not the actresses you see in glossy magazines, not the VIPs, but people like me and my friends, who are often nothing like the image of Italians people expect to see. Italian lifestyle is genuine, easy-going and can be enormously fulfilling. These smiles I quoted earlier, these signals, this welcoming atmosphere, the charm and imagination and strength of our people, is what makes Italy what it is now. An ancient country looking towards the future with confidence and strength.

Surely, the millions of people who choose Italy for their holidays, along with the millions of immigrants who want to live there are both clear indicators of our popularity. Lots of immigrants still see Italy as a sort of Mecca where everything is good, where the sun always shines and where you can find a lovely life for your family. Never mind the corruption, the bureaucracy, the political instability; the image of Italy seems to get better somehow. More and more books are written on living and working in Italy, *La Dolce Vita*, finding a job in Italy, etc, so, it's clear that, with all our faults, we do remain a desirable people living in a desirable country. Italy must be doing well despite all its problems, that is also why we Italians love it so much. And the passion for Italy that shows all over the world is constant proof of this.

As a Sienese living and working in the UK as a journalist I have seen and heard many stories. And I have a privileged perspective, as, before writing this book, I spent a whole year in Siena after twelve in London, just to make sure I had researched the topic enough. I did not want to leave my home town again, of course, but now that I have, I can see what the beauties of Italy are. Maybe more clearly than ever.

It's worth pointing out that there are two different sides of Italy in me: from my mother the Tuscan side, from my father the Neapolitan. That is a bit like saying that I come from two countries. Italy's regions are famously very strongly defined, the country as a whole itself being a relatively young nation. And, to quote Severgnini again, 'it's the kind of place that can have you fuming and then purring in the space of a hundred metres, [over] the course of ten minutes.' So that is why I am writing this book: to take you on an exciting journey through the appealing Italy and the appalling Italy, as Severgnini says, 'the only workshop in the world that can turn out both Botticellis and Berlusconis'.

Part 1 -
What It Means to be Italian
(and How the World Sees Us)

1. Le Tre Italie: Why not to trust geography books

'Abbiamo fatto l'Italia, adesso dobbiamo fare gli Italiani.'
(We have made Italy, now we have to make the Italians.)

– Massimo d'Azeglio, prime minister, in 1870

A SENTENCE STILL VALID SOMEHOW, AFTER OVER A hundred-and-thirty years. In fact, if you ask an Italian where he's from, he will say: Genova, or Napoli, or mention his tiny village in the Alps. Because that is how he feels, he feels he belongs to his region, and to his town, more than to his country.

Before 1861 Italy didn't exist. This was the year it became a nation, while the Italian Republic is even younger: it was voted by referendum just sixty years ago in 1946.

In 2008 we celebrate the sixtieth anniversary of our Constitution, signed on 1 January 1948. Of course, before 1861, the peninsula was heavily featured in history books for its great civilizations and important names and families in the history of Europe, but it just wasn't a country on the map. Instead you could find the Granducato di Toscana and Regno delle Due Sicilie (Granduchy of Tuscany and Reign of the Two Sicilies), and other interesting names, along with towns like Rome, Venice, Pisa and Genova which had been important for many reasons. So Italy was, and somehow still is, a collection of civilizations and languages.

Some of these peoples, while overall feeling Italian, like the idea of keeping their traditions separated from the rest of our nation; this is why some regions have independent movements. Just to mention one, Sardinia has been fighting to be an independent republic for a long time, it publishes magazines and books in its own language to promote the idea of a Repubrica De Sardigna and considers itself a separate entity.

The Italian regions have very strong powers. In fact, there are different laws and different organisation in each region, which reinforce the way in which each of us feels more Tuscan or Milanese or Sardinian than Italian. 'There is little that really links Turin and Bari, or Naples and Trieste, except the *autostrada*, the rail network and the Catholic church', writes Martin Solly, stressing this century-long fact. They say we don't have a national identity, and in some ways this may be true: now that I live abroad, I notice every day how some

Italian mothers don't feel Italian enough to teach their language or traditions to their children, who will learn maybe some words of dialect, but won't ultimately be bilingual. Somehow the fact of having strong regions, with distinct traditions and powers, might have affected the way we think of ourselves. And having a lot of political corruption, and the wrong people representing us abroad, has made it difficult for us to be proud to be Italian. Thank God we won the World Cup. Now at least we wear the footballers' T-shirts and feel proud of the Tricolore flag. Also, thanks to a certain German, we got back to being proud of our engineering and motoring industry: the Schumacher era with Ferrari was legendary and gave us an ego boost – Raikonnen is also very promising indeed.

After the union of Italy, smaller nationalisms and independent movements were born, or became even stronger. Regions like Trentino Alto Adige belonged to Austria until the First World War, and only became Italian during this period. The independent movements of this region, like the Stieler Group, the BAS (Befreiungsauschuss Sudtirol) and the Bib, led by some of the German-speaking population, became a terrorist group in the 1960s. Actions of terrorism and killings were particularly common during these years and didn't stop until the end of the 'seventies. There is still is quite a strong independent tendency today. Sicily and Sardinia also feel independent from Italy: for many years there has been a project to build a bridge over the Stretto di Messina to join the island to the peninsula, but the Sicilians don't really see it as a priority to be directly linked to Italy. In Sardinia, as mentioned, there is a strong will to form an independent republic even now, while in parts of the North, the existence of strong dialects in Veneto and Lombardy inspired independent movements in the 1980s and 1990s.

These are often linked to the variety of languages we still find in Italy: article six of our constitution sanctioned the official use of French in the Val d'Aosta region, and German and Ladino are official languages in Trentino Alto Adige, while Slovene was established by the same article as the language of Gorizia and Trieste. Over the years this town has been contended by the former Yugoslavia, Austria, Germany and Slovenia. In the Cold War, it was divided into Zone A, governed by the USA and the UK, and and Zone B, controlled by Yugoslavia. In 1953 the town was almost a cause of conflict between Yugoslavia and Italy, but finally a treaty restored Trieste to Italy, although part of the town was claimed by Slovenia after its independence. It has only been an Italian town since October 1954.

But separatist movements have never stopped completely in Italy. In very recent years, Padania was founded: a region in the North which covers broadly the Pianura Padana area and spreads further, and for some is a region morally separated from Italy. We even have a political Party, Lega Nord, which is quite popular. It argues for the independence of Padania and campaigns for Europe to be composed of single regions, not countries: of course, according to this party, Italy also should be made up of independent regions.

For historical reasons, to this day there are in fact three Italys: the North driven by money, power and celebrity; the Centre by art, history and tradition; the South by stronger family structures and by ancestral values.

But mainly, the 'southern question', *il Mezzogiorno*, perceived by the other regions as a third-world Italy, has been for centuries a cause of division. Although now things have partially changed, the Southern regions still are a completely different Italy, physically, socially and economically. Films like *Io non ho paura* or *Respiro*, distributed in the UK in recent years, have portrayed this aspect of our country with poetry as well as sadness. Living conditions in the South can be harsh, and the mentality of some parts of it can still be quite far from modern. Some areas seem to have been forgotten by the state and by progress, and there is a general feeling of discomfort in some small areas of Campania, Basilicata and Calabria, where employment is still seven times lower than the average Italian region. This is something I am familiar with, all my father's family being from the South. Now I love the South, its warmth and beauty and the kindness of its people, but often, when I was a child and then in my teens, I was so influenced by the stereotypes I heard around me that I could only see negative sides. Thank God I got over that and I can now see all the beauty and warmth of the region and its people.

It's difficult to ignore, though, that for a long time the North and Centre of Italy felt a strong racism against people coming from the South – comparable to the one some people still feel against foreigners in my country. My family itself was in fact at the centre of a lot of gossiping when my mother got engaged to a 'Neapolitan'.

In Tuscany, in the North and everywhere 'North of Rome', a Southern person was, unfortunately, often seen as lazy, dirty, unreliable and barely literate. So somebody coming from Puglia or Campania, Sicily or even Abruzzi had to pass many tests before being accepted into a Northern family.

My father Cosimo, a decent, handsome, hard-working young man, came to Tuscany to look for a job, following his brother who had already moved to Siena. When he met my mother, of course a scandal exploded. Firstly, he was four years younger than her, the only daughter of a well-to-do family of land owners, then he was a *'terrone'* (a term derived from 'earth', *terra*, which possibly means 'earth eater'), a *'meridionale'* (the common word for 'southerner' but often charged with negative connotations). There was an expression going round in the Fifties and Sixties: 'There should be a wall just below Rome, to keep them all down there'. According to some, the problem was just this: the *Meridionali* did escape and arrived to the North. My father was one of them.

Apparently, even my great-grandfather and one of my great-uncles found it difficult at first to accept what was going on. But they all ended up loving him dearly well before he got engaged to my mum, charming and reliable as he of course was. When I came along, though, I somehow became influenced by this general mentality I felt in the village, and when I was two or three, people used to love asking me who I was and where I was from. Because they got always this answer: 'Annalisa Coppolaro, Lupompesi, Murlo, Siena, *e sono italiana, e napoletana no!'* (and I am Italian, not Neapolitan!). A formula everybody found satisfying and really funny. To make me cross, some of my Tuscan relatives went on a bit about the fact that I had a Southern father, and my raven-black hair didn't help at all, of course. So, being a good Tuscan-Neapolitan, as soon as I could talk, I decided to take the matter into my own hands, so to speak: tantrums before trips to the South, opposition to being kissed by my Southern aunties, and NO learning of the dialect, which I declared I could not understand (this got me out of trying to be nice to my uncles and aunts). I was from Siena, Tuscany, not from Down There, that was all!

A phenomenon directly linked to our regionalism is *'campanilismo'*: we do not just feel we belong to a region or to a town, but to our own *'campanile'*, the bell-tower. And in some villages there is more than one.

In mine, Lupompesi, for example, strictly speaking there isn't a *campanile*, but we are still *Lupompesini*. And we are the cultural elite (after all, engineers, musicians, journalists and bankers live here). We do not much care for the other villages in the area, Casciano and Vescovado, which are historically enemies, as each thinks they are better than the other one.

So each of them keeps their Carnival separate, and they put a lot of energy into holding the best fête and the most exciting football tournament. Recently, they have agreed that this sounds a bit medieval: bear in mind that we are not talking here of a large territory: Murlo, which is the name of the *comune*, or district, comprises now about two thousand people (the population was smaller before, but now a few families have arrived from the Balkans). At the moment, to overcome divisions (!!!), there are women's groups trying to organise fêtes and events for the two villages together, but identity is still kept very distinct, obviously. And those from Vescovado who marry in Casciano, or the other way round, tend to be seen still as quite original, possibly even a bit mad, for marrying outside the borders.

Campanilismo is not all bad: wonderful things have come out of it. For example the Palio horse race. Seventeen *campanili* for seventeen *contrade*, or areas of the city, racing against each other every year, ten at a time, on bare horseback. It's the most sublime horse race you will ever see, in Piazza del Campo: since the Middle Ages, every year, the colours, costumes and emotions are so powerful they can really blow you away.

Each *contrada*, with a couple of exceptions, has a rival, and there are two objectives in the race: win and keep the enemy *contrada* from winning. Families composed of people from different *contrade* split up for several days if the *contrade* all race in the Palio, then they go back to normal after the horse race, (unless the *contrada* of a family member wins the race, in which case that person won't be seen at home for days or weeks – but will come back home to sleep). My great friend Paola from Siena has a twelve-year old daughter whom she hardly saw for a month after her *contrada* won the August 2007 *palio*. But, because a *contrada* is a safe place to be, where there are friends and family, parents don't get worried, but, on the contrary, they feel happy when their child's *contrada* wins.

Mainly, people are truly puzzled when they come to Siena for the first time. They struggle to understand how people can cry and faint and go mad for their own *contrada*, 'all for a three-minute race'. But the Palio is much more, it's the triumph of campanilism, of the pride of belonging to a *contrada*. This is like a second family to the Sienese, a group of people that meet often, organise events together, meet all year long to dine, discuss, get baptised or married. Our young boys don't dream of becoming footballers, but of wearing the glorious colours of the *contrada* in the *campo*, a dream that can lead to tears of happiness when it's fulfilled.

Sociologists say that the reason why Siena has had the lowest crime rate in Italy for ages is due to this powerful magnet that keeps the young linked with each other and interested in the life of their own group, who love and hate and struggle to see the victory of their colours, and who come together to play sports, to have parties, to share interests and daily life. The feeling of belonging to a second enlarged family, who understand and support you, is overpowering for these young people and has a connecting effect that is hard to understand unless you live in our magical town.

This doesn't happen in other towns. That is also why we feel so special and unique, because, at least in Italy, this way of life is only to be found in Siena.

2. The Italians and their families - A love-hate relationship

'The family is far and away the most important social, economic, organisational and political unit in Italy.'

— Martin Solly

ITALIANS FIND IT HARD TO BELIEVE THAT IN BRITAIN, America and other countries children of seventeen are sent off to university and asked to get a loan if they want to study. We look in amazement at families who send their elderly relatives to a home just because they are deemed not useful to society anymore. But are we the only people left to think this? Probably not.

The world talks about how the Italians and other Mediterranean people still believe in family values. We still get married with big parties, have family holidays and celebrate first communions and baptisms with large family gatherings that bring joy and keep relations together. But how much of this is real commitment and how much is a sense of obligation or convenience? How much do we really love our families and how much do they represent a burden?

Hard to say, really. Here we need to look at the regions again. Starting from the South, we can say that, there, family ties are a basic value (and what is *Mafia* if not loyalty to the 'family'?). It's true: people do work and save for wonderful wedding ceremonies, and still look after their old people, divorce is rare here and it still has the stigma of shame attached to it. Religion still has a grip on people, and the idea of family unity is very, very important.

Let's go now to the Centre of Italy. Here, from Rome to Bologna, things are slightly different. Divorcing is not a crime anymore. It's even OK to have 'badanti'; ladies from East Europe who help us look after our grandparents, whom the great majority of families want to keep at home with them. The idea of putting your father in a home is still considered quite shameful, so you can often find enlarged families here: the grandparents, the parents, the children, who might be over thirty but still living at home. The same happens in the North, although, given that the economical situation is even better there, independence is sometimes sought earlier.

I discussed family life with some of my friends in Siena and Florence who are over thirty, have degrees and careers, but are still happily living with their parents. The majority of them replied something like: '*Ma scusa, chi me lo fa fare di andare via?*' ('Sorry, but where is the convenience in leaving home?'). Yes, because if you have a mamma who cooks for you and does your laundry, and gives you support for your problems if you have any, but leaves you the freedom to bring home your girlfriends from time to time, then ... why not? You don't have to pay rent there, you don't have to worry about running a house or paying the bills … and, as people get married in their thirties now, the parents' home looks like the ideal solution until it's time to build a new family.

Things, though, are getting more complicated now. Today, as Paul Ginsborg noted, relationships between children and their parents don't depend so much on emancipation from the family itself: it's got more to do with emancipation within the family (*Modern Day Italy*, 1998).

An important study by Istituto Iard was recently published about what is called the 'young generation' (15–34 year olds) in Italy, now on the website AffariItaliani.

It looks like forty per cent of them live at home with their parents until thirty-four, and seventy-seven per cent find a job at thirty or over, which is the average age to have a family. If we look at the 20–30 age group, the percentage of the young living at home goes up to seventy per cent. Nobody finds it strange in Italy, while many foreigners consider our family structure a bit 'unusual', to put it mildly.

But to understand why people are getting married and starting careers later we should be looking at many other elements. Long university courses, a lack of jobs, and a tendency to have fun for longer and 'grow up' later than the youngsters in other countries are major considerations.

But there are more elements that can't be figured out. After all, Italy has never been very predictable, and our family has been changing over the years. As Flavia Laviosa wrote in her article 'The Post-Modern Italian Family', tradition and modernity seem to live together in a constant dialogue where the relationships inside the family itself point towards new models of family.

It has been said that Italy is a country made of interesting, aggressive over-sixties who have a considerable positive impact on our economy: they still work, travel a lot, know the good things in life and have fun. In fact, once the children have got married, these parents enjoy their freedom. But, if in other countries that happens when you are maybe fifty, here everything is shifted, even the so-called syndrome of the empty nest. People grow up later, and are still considered young at forty, so the Italian sixty-year-olds are in fact only middle-aged and enjoy working, going out and travelling a lot more than in other countries.

As a consequence, old age starts later, people retire later, and, in politics, the media, society in general, there is less space for the young, it seems, as the older refuse to give up. Italy, with a very low birth rate and long life expectancy, is getting older.

As Ian Fisher points out in his article in *The New York Times* that sparked a great deal of debate in Italy, our ageing population is visible everywhere, from television to politics: our presenters, as well as our politicians, are getting older, and both Prodi and Berlusconi are around seventy years old.

The structure of the family is slowly changing in some other ways. On one side, there is a growing number of smaller families, especially in Northern towns, on the other large families are appearing again. These patterns can be linked to a relatively new mentality, where splitting up is not a sin anymore.

Recently on the national RAI2 channel, during a quiz, a lady called, they asked her her age, she said: 86. She then went on talking about the children and grandchildren and great-grand children. 'My son is sixty-five and lives with me, he has a sixty-three-year-old wife, a daughter who is forty, divorced with three children of her own, so all together we are seven'. 'Oh, *che bello*!!!', smiled the presenter.

Divorce, but also the constant increase in house prices, has somehow brought many extended families together again: three generations living together to support each other, something that used to happen in the 'fifties. Working single mothers now need all the support they can get with the kids, so they go back to their family home to make things easier, and in fact, everybody takes advantage of this. The children get to stay with the grandparents and learn from them and from their memories, the single parent gets to have some freedom to go out, see friends and work, the grandparents feel useful and can count on this new generation for support should they become ill. They also benefit from the companionship given by their extended family. In addition to this, there have always been economic schemes connected to the family itself: the idea of the family business, what Flavia Laviosa calls *'famiglia impresa'* is a strong reality in Italy.

The idea of the patriarchal family has changed somewhat, but you will be surprised to see that, again, the split North-South is very strong. So, if in the North older people tend to live by themselves and feel independent, in the South, respect and care for the older people in the family are seen as essential, and hierarchy is almost as important as it used to be in the 'sixties. But things are moving on, and, for a Catholic country, despite a conservative Pope, the freedom of living in a different way has been acknowledged by the institutions.

Laws are changing according to new demands: fewer couples marry, fewer couples have children, more and more families look different, especially in the bigger towns and in the North.

Now there is the *new couple*, you see. Gay or straight couples who want to live together and want more rights and laws to protect them. So, on 12 May 2007, Rome was invaded by one million people for Family Day, a Catholic event organised by the Forum delle Associazioni Familiari. It promoted the traditional family, founded on marriage, and asked the government to keep or make laws accordingly to this aspect of the traditional family. In the next square, still in Rome, a counter-demonstration was organised. The so-called '*Coraggio Laico*', or secular courage, set up a demonstration where gay couples and couples living together tried to show their discontent about a lack of rights for this new aspect of the family. The *Coppia di fatto* couple, not founded on marriage, was trying to have its voice heard.

But, for good or bad, Family still is there, essential and overpowering like no other entity. We care about the judgement of our relatives, we are influenced by their opinions, but, also, we love to be with them.

Large parties, for example, are essential for keeping families together and seem to be a part of everyday Italian culture not mirrored in other European countries. And keeping up appearances, '*fare bella figura*', to show a good figure, as we always say: it's an expression which is not translatable in other languages – it's a bit like showing your best side or sweeping the dust under the carpet. Be perfect, or at least pretend you are (so clean the house when the relatives come over). And if for your child's communion you don't have a large feast in a restaurant, then what will people think?

What about all these young people who swear to hate the duties expected by The Family, only to go back to mamma every time things get tough and every Sunday lunchtime?

So there you go, family is still the pillar of our society. But what do people really feel about this system? Is it a choice or is it a necessity to stay at home with your parents until you are thirty-five?

It varies a lot. I know people who are still living at home

but are building or buying their own place, planning to leave very soon. They have a job and they want independence. Some other 'youngsters' (25–34-year-olds) are struggling to settle down in their jobs and find it cheaper and more practical to live with their parents or grandparents. The housing market hasn't been particularly favourable to first-time buyers and it takes a few years for younger people to build enough money for a property. Unemployment in Italy has gone down a lot in recent years and currently stands at six per cent, but it's also true that short-term contracts are often chosen by an employer when it comes to giving a job to a 'young person'. A very interesting article in N*igrizia* (one of the magazines I work for) tells the story of an African woman in Italy, Igiaba Scego, who says that, at thirty-three, she's very tired of being considered 'young', and wants a proper job, not just short-term agreements. ('N*on sono giovane*', N*igrizia* December 2007.)

But I also have friends who have possibly left it too late to leave their parents, and now the parents are older, their children haven't got the heart to actually find a place for themselves. These, in the eyes of society, are possibly the saddest cases. The sense of duty which is something we are all taught, together with the respect for the elderly and the idea that your parents look after you so you are supposed to look after them, are sometimes paralysing and can prevent people from leading proper independent lives. In times when reaching the age of ninety happens a lot in Italy, it's not uncommon to find fifty-year-olds who are single and look after their parents until they die; I could quote at least four cases in my family. What people should understand is that the majority do it because they want to, as a choice, and not because they feel obliged or because society doesn't offer alternatives. Plenty of retirement homes and home-helpers are available.

But in our culture, leaving an older person to die in a home still seems the wrong thing to do. And it's very common for one or two grandparents to live with our partner and children, for example.

More than from religion, I would say that this attitude comes from a certain way of seeing 'the family': the value of 'respect', which seems to be lost in many other contexts and in other countries alike, is still the basis of our relationships with the oldest members of our families. Grandparents, great-uncles, and sometimes even older relatives who are not strictly our blood relations, are often seen as the keepers of traditions, memories and values that need to be upheld and respected. Also, many young people still hold to the idea of 'giving back' the affection that was given to them by their parents and grandparents.

It was very interesting to read some of the 122 comments posted on the Times Online website in response to an article written by Richard Owen in *The Times* ('Mamma's Boys', 8 January 2008). Many Italians from Italy and from the UK answered, as well as people from Australia and the US who wanted to respond to this article, which basically described our men as being unable to cut links with their families and failing in their relationships as a result. Well, some of the comments posted by Italian men and women are quite significant, and say a lot about our idea of family:

Here you find all the love and respect that the Italian people really feel towards their parents, and their attachment to traditional values. "Respect", "gratitude", "love", and very often the desire to raise children with these values emerge from many of these letters. One man wrote, 'I'd rather spend time with my mum than at the pub, after work with my colleagues drinking pints [and] pints. And yes, I still thank my mum for only having taken me to McDonalds maybe once every month.'

Here are two more examples: 'My Italian man loves his espresso (not macchiato), is a high achiever (and not just in bed!) adores me and the kids and, oh, yes, loves his mamma too! I wish my sons will turn out to be like him!'

'... I prefer taking care of my old mother who has done everything for me instead [of throwing] her away in a hospice without any respect or gratitude ...'

I think these words don't need many comments: 'respect', 'sense of family', 'values', but also the division between North and South (and the sense of family being stronger in the South) are quite significant. Some of the men who posted comments greet the reporter with 'Ciao from a Mamma's boy', and they mostly seem very proud of being so. Of course there is the occasional comment admitting that it is too much, that working conditions in Italy mean that we can't become independent until we are over thirty, which is surely one more reason why in some cases we would stay at home instead of moving out. 'From necessity comes virtue', an old Italian proverb goes: and in some cases, our choice to stay lovingly with the family really comes from this aspect of our economy.

But surely 'passion and a strong sense of values', as a reader from Florence says in response to the article, are the basis of our family relationships, and, as another woman married to an Italian man added, 'this loving family environment nurtured a self assured, considerate human being who has the utmost respect [for] women. Perhaps a woman who rarely expresses her love and regularly packs her children off to McDonalds, rather than spend thirty minutes in the kitchen, would have produced one of the fine young men we see stumbling out of Britain's pubs today.'

So, it's true, also according to those who live with Italians or know Italy, that a different code of values and a more spontaneous way of expressing our feelings do make a difference in our country. We have a humanity rarely found elsewhere.

All these irate answers to Owen's article are not written by chance: they are also the result of a social world that in Italy still puts the emphasis on family and on its importance.

But things are not always as straightforward as you think: love and a sense of duty can be linked and in some cases they can cripple your life if you become a slave to duty itself.

So, if on one hand we often feel the necessity of looking after our elderly relatives, on the other hand it can have its drawbacks. My experience is that many other factors come into play, depending on circumstance: your own conscience, your values, your fear of being judged.

I have a direct experience of how hard it can be to have such a strict code of values regarding our families. My mother lives with us, for example, and this is very positive in many ways: we can go out in the evenings without worrying about babysitting, of course and I can work when the kids are at home as they are with my mum. The children also gain so much as they are learning many things from her past, listening to her memories and sharing her experiences. I lived at home until I was almost twenty-seven and it didn't occur to me, or to my friends who were doing the same, that we would have more freedom if living somewhere else. I remember being fed up with the limitations I had to endure when I was a teenager (back from parties by midnight, no sexy clothes, no sleeping away from home unless on holidays with friends or on school trips etc), but then again, when I started to drive, I was freer to move around and I always managed to find a compromise. But when I left Italy to come to live in the UK with my husband, it was perceived as radical. You don't just leave your family after taking your degree: they have looked after you and paid for your studies, and then, as a thank you, you leave them? So I was a seriously bad girl. The other problem was that, being an only child, I was leaving my parents by themselves to look after the farm and my eighty-year-old grandparents. Which you are not supposed to do. I don't think I was ever forgiven for this, possibly not until I went back to live in Italy for a year with my husband and children and after deciding that we will return to live in Tuscany at some time in the future.

Nico Tulini, one of the people I interviewed about our tendency to live at home with our parents until our thirties wrote:

'There are mainly two reasons for the young people not to leave their parents' house. One is 'mamma': the mothers don't want to lose their children and are ready to be slaves to their kids forever. When a son or a daughter leaves there is a feeling of loss comparable to the death of a loved one. The other reason is linked to our economy: the dual problem of low wages and temporary jobs that influences the choice of staying at home.' In recent years there has been a tendency in Italy to give young people contracts for part-time jobs or temporary jobs, as per the short contract system, giving people the chance to work but for lower wages. The Prodi government has made changes and it has become easier to get employment and better conditions. As for universities, before the recent reform, nobody could get a degree before they were twenty-five, but mostly the average age for finishing university was twenty-seven or over. I was quick and got my degree at twenty-six (I was also doing journalism work). Now things have changed and students are ready to start working at an earlier age. 'Often the people who choose to study at a university that is far from home are more prone to leave the parents' home, while those who go straight into work are often at home until they find a partner or get married. The high cost of renting and buying homes in general are another important factor.'

Nico, who is a lawyer, also added that often people don't want to move as each small village or town has its own habits, dialect, food: so we feel like strangers when we travel too fast. He also had interesting ideas regarding another habit in Italy which we will describe in the sex chapter, and which doesn't exist in other countries of Europe.

Massimo, just like Nico, pointed out that we don't feel ashamed at all in remaining at our parents' homes when we are older than twenty-five. Massimo in fact lived with his parents until he was about thirty and many of his friends did the same. In my circle of friends, we all left home when we got married, and those who didn't found a house for themselves at about thirty-five. No sense of guilt or anything … and of course, no rent! I have neighbours in London who pointed out that their children, in their twenties, still live at home since they can't find a flat. But they pay rent, of course!

So, living at home for us is a tradition, really, and nobody finds it surprising in Italy. Only the foreigners do.

3. The Voices - How we feel about ourselves: Interviewing the Italians

'In Italy for thirty years under the Borgias they had warefare, terror, murder and bloodshed but they produced Michelangelo, Leonardo da Vinci and the Renaissance. In Switzerland, they had brotherly love; they had five hundred years of democracy and peace and what did that produce? The cuckoo clock.'

– Orson Welles

ARE WE PROUD OF BEING ITALIAN OR IS THE BAD press we sometimes get influencing our view of who we are and how much we are worth? Have the Berlusconi years been messing with our self-respect?

What do we think of ourselves? A good question. Generally, especially in recent years, the Italians seem to take a special pleasure in undermining their country.

It's a strange phenomenon, and might still be related to our regional sense.

If we are Neapolitan or Piedmontese, you won't hear us

criticise our '*corregionali*', in fact we'll praise our region and all its traditions, history and food but we will happily describe our country as a land of corruption and mafia and deceit, where things don't work, a land, ultimately, made up more and more of foreigners, pigs and tarts.

It's a sort of morbid pleasure that all Italians have, and it's also fashionable among writers: books are published on this very idea, just for the sake of proving that no other nation is as bad, as corrupt and as horrid as Italy, and no population is composed of more lying cheats than ours.

Fortunately, it's not true, but it sells very well.

Italians do have good hearts, warm personalities and a loving disposition most of the time. They know how to enjoy themselves and they are able to find the good things even in a bad situation.

A lot of films were produced in the Neorealism period about this idea: while things went wrong around them the main characters of the films did manage to survive and make the best of their qualities, thus improving their situation and turning the bad into good. Some great examples are *Pane, Amore e Fantasia*, in which Gina Lollobrigida's character lives in a tiny village , her life is very poor but she manages to buy things cheaply by flirting with the shopkeepers, and her life is improved greatly when she gets married to a *Carabiniere* of the village. There are also iconic films directed by Vittorio de Sica like *L'Oro di Napoli* in which Sophia Loren plays a pizza maker managing to survive thanks to her shrewd way of tricking the law. But perhaps the best of all is *Ieri, Oggi e Domani*, again directed by de Sica, where Loren plays a fish seller who has trouble with the law. To avoid going to prison she keeps on having children, since they couldn't put her behind bars when pregnant or breastfeeding.

'We turn a crisis into a party' this very basic idea, mentioned earlier, is important in our way of life, and we're known for it all over the world. The characters in the neorealistic films often sing, smile and seem happy enough: a way to trick destiny.

Some of our best creations came out of a crisis. Think of pizza; they say it was invented when a renaissance cook found that he only had flour, salt, water and tomatoes available to make a meal. So he invented possibly the most famous Italian dish of all times.

When you think that our country has gone though many difficult moments but is still one of the most admired and envied all over the world, then you will understand that we have always been extremely good at *arte di arrangiarsi* – the art of getting by. An art, yes, as getting by can become a wonderful opportunity, if approached with intuition, cleverness and creativity. Our sense of enterprise, also, is very useful in overcoming some of the difficult situations Italy finds itself in; sometimes producing some very funny ideas.

When the government decided to make seatbelts compulsory in 1989, a lot of people, especially in the South, found the price of seatbelts and the work to put them in place much too high. In Naples – so the story goes – some of the city's enterprising inhabitants came up with the ideal solution: as it was summertime, they invented the 'seatbelt shirt'. Basically, instead of spending 500,000 liras to fit seatbelts in your car, you could just spend 10,000 and buy yourself a T-shirt with a black seatbelt painted on it. Apparently the police at first fell for it, and the creators of the T-shirt made some money for at a least a few days!

Of course, we would all be happier with better politics, better employment and a better society, where nobody gets killed at football matches and where we won't be ridiculed

23

for having naked girls in our ads and for our female politicians showing off their legs in a miniskirt. This is the kind of thing the media loves: Italy as a country where advertising agencies use naked bodies to sell all sorts of products, its housewives take off their clothes on TV and its women politicians are virtually porn-stars.

But it's important to understand that our culture *is* different: no TV channel in the UK or the US would show Italian ads, and feminists are outraged by how women are often scantily clad in shows, even when they have a position of power in society. In reality our behaviour is much more innocent than it appears on TV. It is, again, more of a light-hearted approach to showing beauty from different angles. An article by Adrian Michaels, published in *The Financial Times* ('Naked Ambition', 13 July 2007) contains an interview with a young fashion student who points out that often, for us, nudity is connected to beauty. And for ordinary women, as well as for female politicians or actresses, wearing a short skirt on TV is a way to show that they are still beautiful and well-preserved.

My generation has in fact grown up in a changing environment, and I do believe that we all feel this quite strongly. On one side, we had the influence of the Church telling us what to do, on the other different influences like feminism, the sexual revolution, first contraceptives and the legalisation of abortion – all of which began when we were just small children, but of course affected all of us by the time we reached our teens. Somehow, we all are the product of these many factors, so on one side, as women, we want to appear progressive and modern, on the other side we think that affirming our sexiness through revealing clothes is our right. For example, if you visit any administrative office in Italy, you will be struck by the way women dress at work.

Miniskirts, animal prints and see-though shirts are not at all uncommon among employees, even the very highly qualified, all over Italy, and only a fraction use the classically cut suit that seems to be typical business attire for women in other parts of the world. But in spite of our seemingly flamboyant dress sense, we are as highly professional as our European neighbours.

When my brother-in-law came from Wales to assist me in some office matters in Italy while my husband was looking after the kids, he was struck by two things: the impressive efficiency and humanity of the staff in all the offices we visited, and the way people at work dress. The efficiency was somehow unexpected (we know that abroad people believe Italy is very slow in bureaucratic matters), and the look some employees showed off was somehow unexpected too. In fact men, often, just like women, don't go for the shirt and tie, for example, but like to show off their body with tight shirts and trousers.

A sexier style in the workplace is a natural part of the Italian attitude to beauty and self-image: the English phrase 'if you've got it flaunt it' would apply to many of us, as we think that what counts in the workplace is the work we do and not what we wear. Obviously, we also think that dressing in an interesting way can be comfortable and can lighten up the most boring jobs: it's part of making the most of our daily life.

All of this is reflected by our TV shows of course, and by gossip magazines. Our culture is just very different from that of many other countries all over the world. And most of us don't find anything wrong in our love of showing off a bit.

But how does Italy really perceive itself at present? To understand more precisely the way we see ourselves, I decided to interview the Italians. When I wrote my book on fidelity, friends asked if I had done a lot of research … I had, but not of the bed-jumping kind. I had asked many people from different age groups and with differing beliefs what they thought of this value. This turned out to be very enlightening. I realised how much people varied and how it's easy to generalise, too easy. It seems, generally, that being faithful is still an important value, just like in other parts of the world, but of course there are also people who think they have to be faithful but that oral sex does not count! In some of the results of this survey in fact I realised that for some people, mainly men, only the complete sex act represents true infidelity, while kissing, petting or oral sex are often considered half-infidelities.

Papers and books try to prove that the Italians don't think much of themselves. I personally don't really believe that all Italians consider themselves a bunch of horrid, untrustworthy people. Living abroad helps you have a different, wider perspective, so I decided to create two questions, the first: 'How would you describe the Italians – good or bad?' And the second: 'Why do you think the world is so interested in us?' This was essential in order to see what separates us from other populations – or at least what the Italians think about this and to really prove that in fact we do love ourselves, despite our tendency to complain about the political and social problems in our country. I put these questions to a sample of people ranging from their twenties to their seventies, and the results are quite interesting. I also used www.italiansoflondon.com, where I posted a question about the fascination that the English-speaking world seems to have with Italy. The answers were brilliant:

'We are a population of contrasts. White and black, good and bad, progress and obscurantism: a country that has the Pope, lots of people who believe in black magic, the mafia, the best art and culture, the best design in the world, people with loving, sunny eyes who welcome you and want to share things with you, lots of genuine people but also cheating people who are able to build the worst scams imaginable … Italians are incredible. That is why I miss them so much.' A declaration of love and hate from one of the people who answered my questions, Elisa, who is working in London for three years but wants to go back.

There seem to be two dominant national characteristics that make Italians truly Italian: *'simpatia'*, and having a sense of beauty and style. *'Simpatia'*, 'being simpatico' (another Italian word that has made its way into the English language): a person who is *'simpatica'* is nice, funny, charming, and gets along with people. I remember it was one of the first things I asked my husband when I met him. I had a good grasp of English but the exact nuances of this word eluded me. He said we could possibly translate it also as 'nice'… but nice does not cover it, really. Somebody could be not nice at all and be really *simpatico*. In fact, some Italian criminals are extremely *simpatici* and capture your imagination immediately.

Italians can laugh, too, and *'sdrammatizzare'* (lighten things up) even in the hardest moments. Our best films and our best actors are the comic ones, from Roberto Benigni to Alberto Sordi, from Carlo Verdone to Silvio Muccino.

Again, there are regional differences: some regions are more simpatico than others – and Tuscany, it seems, wins, possibly because of the accent. 'In Tuscany we are slightly more fun and simpatici than in other regions,' 'Nicola Ulivieri writes, 'maybe because of our culture or our accent which people find amusing everywhere. One other characteristic is the fact of not taking things too seriously. For example, as Benigni says, we use swearing as a way of livening up the sentence…'

And then, of course, there's the other thing we're known the world over for: our sense of beauty and style. TV motoring shows often use the phrase, as much as it could become a cliché, when reviewing the latest Italian cars. But there is truth in it.

We pay great attention to the way we look and dress, we like choosing the right colours and materials, and we go to a lot of trouble to appear better than the people around us. That is why our parties are such a feast for the eyes: even in other countries and cities, if you go to an Italian party, people look beautiful and smart and the décor is usually brilliant. Would this be part of *'far bella figura'* (making a good impression)? Of course: you always need to be perfect for the occasion. 'Italians always take great care to wear the right clothes on the right occasion. This is never a casual choice – it is important to wear the proper clothes for the role you are playing', writes Martin Solly in his book *The Xenophobe's® Guide to the Italians*, taking things a step further he underlines the Italians' love of uniforms: 'The station master must look like a station master. He must act the part too since he's on stage in the great film set of life'.

Our love for theatre and melodrama could have something to do with this. But also our idea of beauty, which is famous all over the world. Our sense of style has been criticised sometimes as overpowering: some say we are more interested in appearing than in being. Hard to say if it's true: one could argue that we are just less restrained than other people, and more in touch with our natural human exuberance! However you look at it, it's an indisputable fact that the Italians have produced a huge amount of great works of art and architecture, (and even a few good cars!) even in recent years. Evidence of how highly regarded Italian art and architecture have long been can be seen in the finest buildings, gardens and galleries around the world.

Paradoxically, you can find the opposite of these two qualities everywhere.

We can be extremely heavy and *antipatici*, we can tend to see things worse than they are, and we can be the opposite of welcoming if you get us on the wrong day.

And, while creating arguably the best buildings in the world, sometimes we are also confronted with inefficiency. Some of our regions are dotted with reminders of the beginnings of what were meant to be great works with ambitious plans ... but then the money runs out and the towns are left with decaying eyesores in the middle of what were lovely spaces. Francesco, who took part in my survey, wrote: 'We are unsatisfied and frustrated, even if we have everything we want, the car, the house, the work, the family. We are never happy...' And Antonio Vigni added:'We are the least scrupulous of people, we are full of debts...We all think we are sexy, but having charm is an individual quality, either Mother Nature has given it to you or it's useless to try...'

There was also a third question I sent to some of those who replied to the first two: '*How is it that in Italy we are able to 'live better' than in other countries?*'

The answer is 'dynamism and adaptability'. Almost every response underlined this quality, which can turn into *arte di arrangiarsi*, the aforementioned art of getting by.

Traditionally, the Italians seem good at surviving and even making the best of a country that is quite complicated. This is also possibly the key to their success abroad; they have the gift of adapting to different conditions, often being used to doing just that in Italy of course.

'Anything can happen to them' – Umberto Genovese writes – 'either in the government, in culture, fashion or sport, and

they can turn it into a curious mix which helps them get by…
That is why they can live better than others…'

For some it's a matter of mental flexibility:

'If a thing should be done this way, but the Italian sees
that it's better to do it his or her way, then Italians take their
own decisions and choose to behave in an unpredictable
way, finding his own answer to the problem. They don't look
at the instruction booklets, they take things into pieces
instead, that is why you never find instruction booklets in
the Italian language when you buy something!' (Flavio
Borgogni).

'I believe that our main positive side is the way of always
looking for an optimum lifestyle, and our search for beauty
as an ideal background for our daily actions,' added Simone
Berni, 'also, we work to live, we do not live to work!' – a
sentiment that our friend Martin Solly also observes in his
Xenophobe's® Guide to the Italians.

So, after work the real fun starts: meeting friends and
going out, without over-indulging in alcohol or drugs, but
just for the pleasure of taking the good things in life:
friendship, love, food. It's widely known how much the
Italians value friendship – it's as important as food! Far from
it being a cult, as some have said, eating well is a major part
of our daily life, whether we're at home or away.

'The British like our lifestyle because…we have the better
cuisine in the world!' commented Giovanna Plebani, who
runs a cookery school at her home in the UK, 'I can read it
in the English people's eyes: they love eating a pasta done
properly, they find it a sublime experience!'

So, we do really live better, in Italy … or do we?

An interesting theory is that Italians THINK they live
better. Nicoletta Sinatti said:

'Being convinced that they *are* better, they think they live

30

better because they are Italians! I don't think they do comparisons with other people, they are just convinced… So they think they eat better, cook better, dress better, have better women, better jobs…'

Now, this can be interpreted in different ways, but it's surely a revealing factor about the way we see ourselves: we think we are attractive and have quite a healthy self-esteem that is regarded by some as out of place. Many Italians believe they are capable of achieving the best life possible in a country that has had problems in the past and can still be difficult. Also, a good number of people said: 'We live better because we know how to stay together and have friends.' The idea of stopping in the street to speak to friends, socialising, saying 'hello' and having a joke or a small conversation, even during working hours, being sunny and smiley and welcoming to each other and to those who come to Italy seem to be part of our nature. In this case, it's about disposition more than anything else. In the same research into the 15–34 year olds, the list of values that are important in this age group are, in order: health, family, peace, freedom, love and friendship. So keeping our love and friendship and family links alive is a very high priority for many of us.

This is possibly why visitors who come to Italy, from North to South, want to come back, and also, as Severgnini writes, 'People who live in Italy say they want to get out, but those who do escape all want to come back … As you will understand, this is not the sort of country that is easy to explain…'

4. Italiani Brava (e Bella) Gente: Italy in the World

'There is an underlying generosity in Italy that we Americans are losing ... Italian generosity is also evident in other attitudes that you may not notice anymore. We do. There's the absence of chauvinism, the self-criticism, and the almost childlike inquisitiveness toward others. You don't just look at people in Italy; you see them.'

– from a letter by American readers sent to the writer Beppe Severgnini – published in his book La Bella Figura

ITALIANS GOOD (AND BEAUTIFUL) PEOPLE: A GAME of words based on the famous expression 'Italiani brava gente', a famous film by Giuseppe De Santis (1965) now also a blog on MySpace all for Italians and a website (www.italianibravagente.com).

It was probably the film, a beautiful work of art set in Second-World-War Italy, which used this expression first. But the good nature, wit, warmth and generosity of the Italians are not just proverbial. We may struggle in some fields as a country, but we have managed to keep smiling, hoping and being happy – in the Berlusconi era and in the Prodi era. It's simply our nature. And we welcome foreigners, whether they want to come to live in Italy, or just want to visit, with open arms.

Despite the articles about rubbish in the streets of Naples and the Pope not being welcome in our universities, we have established that Italy has a good reputation abroad. This is due in part to the talented and charming people carrying Italian names all over the world. So many are the musicians, artists, actors and public figures linked to Italy: last century's tradition is continuing now, with more new names coming into the spotlight.

Who are the Italians who represent us abroad? Pavarotti was one, along with Berlusconi and Sophia Loren. Now of course there's Carla Bruni, Monica Bellucci, Fabio Capello, to name but a few. Sporting personalities, actresses who steal the hearts of presidents, politicians with doubtful CVs, the greatest soprano in the world: is it because of the media that Italy gets noticed so much? The answer is no.

Even in the Middle Ages and the Renaissance, our VIPs were big news: from Dante to Boccaccio, from Piero della Francesca to Galileo, from Marco Polo to Christopher Columbus, from Leonardo to Michelangelo, through to Alessandro Volta, Guglielmo Marconi and Maria Montessori, arts and culture from Italy spread all over the world inspiring great works and 'advertising' Italy. The bestselling book and subsequent film *The Da Vinci Code* helped reignite a tremendous passion for that period of history where one of our greatest geniuses, Leonardo Da Vinci, managed to design a type of aircraft a few centuries before flight, paint the Mona Lisa and invent the basis for automobiles.

It was another Italian who left Spain to reach a land that

was thought at the time to be India, but it became clear that in fact another continent had been discovered. It was 1492 and Columbus had reached the Bahamas. He went on to land in America in 1498.

We have batteries and radios thanks to Italians like Volta and Marconi, pianos and violins thanks to incredible Italian craftsmanship, opera thrives as a hugely popular genre thanks to our passion for music, perspective in painting was first presented by Piero della Francesca. In science, music, painting, architecture possibly no other country has done as much as Italy for progress. Some argue that this is a thing of the past, that now lots of our best minds will go abroad to find a better environment to express real change. It isn't true: the real creativity and passion that can still be found in our country might not have the signature of Leonardo, but it still has the trademark of our amazing people.

* * *

Indeed, Italians travel. They have exported pasta to China and imported spices from there to Rome. Some of the most famous people in the world are of Italian descent, and they are the people who promote Italy abroad. Cinema and music are the fields in which these Italians excel: Sylvester Stallone, John Travolta, Madonna, Frank Sinatra, Al Pacino, Marlon Brando, Liza Minnelli, Robert De Niro, Francis Ford Coppola, Frank Capra, and more recently Paolo Nutini, Andrea Bocelli and Ludovico Einaudi are all household names, and are showing that Italian origins often mean creativity and charisma. Together with our artists, fashion designers and composers, these are the names that have helped to make Italy a symbol of success and passion.

* * *

How else does Italy contribute to global culture? As we have seen, politics today in Italy does not do much for the country's image. 'Italy is a country which seems to survive despite the efforts of its politicians to ruin it', writes Martin Solly in his *Xenophobe's*® *Guide*. And in a way it's true. Some years ago, the world's press wrote about Ilona Staller, a.k.a. Cicciolina; a porn actress who became famous for her movies but later for the fact she became a member of the Italian Parliament. Pictures of Cicciolina sitting next to her fellow politicians, wearing nearly nothing and smiling her large smile with huge, botox-enhanced, blood-red lips are still fond memories for those Italians who distrust politics and politicians. It was, in a way, a symbol of our corrupt political life at the time, and Berlusconi was viewed by the media as a figurehead for that style of politics.

The papers wrote a lot about his public apology to his wife after he was too flirty with other women. Or, rather, when Veronica very publicly requested an apology from him by writing to the bestselling (left-wing) daily newspaper *La Repubblica*. It was quite an event for the gossip press all over the world. Again, we Italians were puzzling our observers. It's fun, really. Especially because there have also been intelligent women: parliamentary presidents, like Irene Pivetti and Emma Bonino, a member of the European commission who has been fighting against the low image of Italian women in politics and who represents that progressive, post-feminist era some Italian women belong to. In a sense, Romano Prodi represented a new Italy which was fighting to get recognition as a nation that wants change. This is slowly happening, but will take a while to rid our country of its problems. On one hand, of course, our politics haven't been great. On the other hand, there has been a tendency for the press to portray an image, in Italy and abroad, which hasn't exactly been flattering. It will probably take a while before the public perception changes. However, change *is* happening, thanks to some new names in politics, and to a new positive attitude among people.

It is of course easier to highlight the negative aspects of a country that was dominated by mafia and camorra for so long, and still is in a way. The book *Gomorrah*, recently published in its English translation, was written by Roberto Saviano and explores a different sort of mafia, the Neapolitan Camorra, which works in a similar way to the traditional mafia but is less well known. There was much talk about the fact that the British edition didn't include some of the names of the UK bosses – a certain censorship was applied, in Italy as well as in the UK. However, the book generally confirms what the world still thinks of Italy: a country where do-it-yourself law is superior to the institutional judicial system. The book *Modern Italy* by John Foot, also takes this approach, and again gives the impression that too many things are wrong with our country. Undeniable, but it's important to remember that Italy has a great many virtues in spite of its troubled politics and history of organised crime.

Clichès and stereotyping are hard to beat, and the creators of best-selling TV productions know this. *The Sopranos* is arguably one of the most popular US television series of all time. Its final episode was watched by millions of people when it aired in the autumn of 2007. Why such a following? Is it because the show gives a picture of Italians that is very close to the stereotypes people have had in mind for decades? That men are sexy cheating liars who often consider themselves above the law. That women are good cooks and good in bed, have learned not to trust others and deal with their lying, cheating men by spoiling them rotten and turning a blind eye to their obvious faults and infidelities. Essentially, The Sopranos reinforces the idea that in Italy we improvise a lot, we do things our way, we make up for the lack of laws by inventing our own, we often turn to compromise, and we revert to Do It Yourself solutions when there is a vacuum of control.

This is one side of the coin: the other side is Joey Tribbiani, one of the trio of leading men in the equally popular show *Friends*, and the only character to develop into a spin-off series when the long-running show came to an end. For many years, Joey has been a positive symbol of Italy, the face of Young Italy somehow, the typical *ragazzo simpatico* who lives by *arte di arrangiarsi*, who is naïve but clever, clumsy but sexy, unbearably irritating but extremely charming at the same time. Joey wants to become an actor but manages to get only second-class parts: this somehow unlucky quest is very fascinating for girls and makes him the most successful man in the household in a way. He knows how to lie, but he's also cute, intelligent and cuddly; I have met plenty of men like him in Italy.

I think these two faces of the Italian male, represented by the *Sopranos* men and Joey, encapsulate a lot about the image we have abroad.

Interestingly, it's harder to pinpoint female role-models that have been successful in presenting an image of the typical Italian woman to the outside world. Cinema and fashion are usually the only fields where our women attract attention or make the news, with a couple of exceptions. Beauty is the most common quality associated with our women. *Bellissima: Feminine Beauty and the Idea of Italy*, a recent book by Stephen Gundle, a professor of film and television studies and Italian history at Warwick University, sums up very well the way Italian women are perceived by the world. Gundle also points out that this sense of style and beauty seems to be part of our nature and all those women who, down the centuries, have represented Italy abroad (from Queen Margherita to Manuela Arcuri) have a kind of charm that you won't find anywhere else. The dark, protective, mother-like figures with curves, curls and deep, dark eyes are still characteristics that men expect to find in the real Italian woman.

On the subject of the deep connection between Italy and beauty, the blurb on Gundle's book says: 'Feminine beauty has been more discussed, appreciated, represented in art and associated with national, cultural identity in Italy than in any other country.' Towards the end of the book, Gundle states that 'the language employed to describe women in the public domain has evolved little and … for good or ill, female beauty continues to occupy a central place in the national culture'. Charm and beauty are our most celebrated qualities: no doubt about that.

Only recently, *Neighbours*, the popular Australian soap, has introduced two beautiful young Italian sisters in the plot. They are sexy, have style, can cook, get away with things and make men fall in love with them. One of the story-writers, Riccardo Pellizzeri, has an Italian name and he seems to know about our culture, or at least the image Italy has in the world. The two sisters seem to represent the two sides of Italy: one of them, Rosetta, is a serious, hard-working lawyer who gets married and is consistent in her choices. Her sister, Carmella, swings between roles, and even joins a convent for a time, only to discover that it's not the life she wanted. Rosetta and Carmella's father of course is in prison for Mafia-related crimes.

Our image hasn't changed that much it seems … at every latitude and even in the screen writers' imagination. One thing we can safely say about all these Italian characters, both men and women, is that they certainly have *style*. Elegant, classy, beautiful, irresistible even: the typical Italian *has* to be like this. For both men and women, for good or ill, style and beauty are central. Even for Berlusconi and Pavarotti, Boccelli and Prodi, it's necessary to maintain a certain look for the roles they are playing.

Is this why very few people outside of Italy have heard of two of our brilliant scientists – women – who are not young or sexy? These two amazing women are Rita Levi Montalcini, now 98, winner of the Nobel Prize for Medicine in 1986 for her research into growth factors, and Margherita Hack, 70, one of the world's leading astronomers, who is a member of the Royal Astronomical Society and of the International Union of Astronomers.

These women of culture, who have made many scientific discoveries essential for man, who have published many interesting books and are internationally known in their fields, are not stereotypical Italian women. Another woman, Maria Montessori, revolutionised the world of education between the end of the eighteenth century and all though the first half of the nineteenth, and she is possibly the woman of culture for whom the world envies us the most. The idea of self-directed learning she introduced ensured the continuing success of many Montessori schools all over the world. But again she doesn't fit into our glamorous profile, so she is known relatively little.

Our advertising and cinema make the most of Italian women's beauty, and, although the trend is now changing, nudity is quite common in our advertising campaigns. The recent article in *The Financial Times* I quoted earlier reported on the fact that in Milan Airport it's quite common to see girls dressed in very sexy clothes inviting travellers to buy products, from mobile phones to laptops. So we can't really blame anyone for this image we have abroad: we still think that showing off a bit is a natural part of our character, and we like doing it from time to time. The housewife, the professional, the doctor, the student, the civil servant might all think there's nothing wrong in dressing up from time to time. Some women might feel that this is not appropriate for our status in society, but many of us feel fine with it. We don't necessarily feel exploited by men, on the contrary we feel sexy and desired when men look at us in the streets.

We are even proud of it, and proud of our difference, both mental and physical.

In fact, as Stephen Gundle points out, 'still today, Italian femininity , in so far as it is articulated as a national typology, is often counterposed to contemporary visions of beauty that emanate from abroad. While millions of Italian women have embraced lifestyles and roles that are in every way equivalent to those of women in other European countries, the conventional image of the Italian woman as a beautiful, dark-haired, olive-skinned force of nature persists albeit in a much-evolved form. An ideal of naturalness is a key value. [She offers] a vision of sex appeal not as manufactured construct but as a quality that is related to physical being, a particular pattern of gender relations and a relaxed lifestyle.'

So, Italiani brava gente or Italiani bella gente? Are we more 'good' or more 'beautiful' in the eyes of the world? I would say the latter. In my experience, it's still true that the world focuses on what is more brightly-coloured, shiny and visually interesting, or somewhat scandalous and unbeliev-able. Recently so much has been written on Italy, about the love story of Carla Bruni with Sarkozy, and generally about our women conquering international cinema little by little. 'Italiane da export', was a front-page headline in *Panorama* in December 2007, and the article highlighted all these Italian women who in different ways are now conquering the world.

But it's clear that the media are basically scared of breaking away from the same old patterns: clichés sell, people look for them and want to read about them.

Writing that Italy is a nation rich in great minds – not just in the Renaissance but now – wouldn't make the headlines as much as the rubbish in the streets of Naples. So we get to read about mafia and camorra instead.

* * *

Thankfully, our passion for food and for art, fashion, sport, music and design are still the most wonderful things associated with us: they, along with the stars and celebrities we export, are what saves our image abroad.

I want to take you step by step into our world, to show you that we know how to live, we recognise good things, and we are not called *il Bel Paese* for nothing.

It's not just the people, or the climate, or the food, or the beauty and harmony you can find in our land: it's a mixture of all of these things, in different doses. Only knowing all the ingredients will enable you to enjoy life Italian-style to the full.

Forget the bad reviews: *Italiani Brava Gente* can say more than thousands of articles on the press. Take it from one who knows the tricks of the trade! This is why I'm focusing mostly on the good things our country has to offer. When you live in Italy most of the time, you understand that we are truly *Il Bel Paese*, despite the odd scandal and a few clichés.

5. Italians abroad: The Expat and the Holiday-maker

'We choose really impossible destinations so that we can tell our friends about it afterwards'

– Antonio Vigni

'We go on holiday to really plain destinations … no sense of adventure!'

– Nicoletta

LET'S TRY A SMALL QUIZ. SUPPOSE YOU DON'T KNOW our language, and you magically find yourself in a beautiful white, stuccoed room somewhere in the world, with lots of elegant people standing around and greeting each other. Everybody is waiting for something to start. How do you know you are at an Italian event? If the men wear beautifully cut suits and expensive watches, if the women are classy without being over the top. If the event was meant to start twenty-five minutes ago but still nothing happens, if everybody is greeting each other saying: '*Caro commendatore* ...' or '*Dottor Rossi, quanto tempo* ...'. If people are smiling cordially and seem to be at ease with each other, if finally the event starts and the spoken introduction goes on for hours. If a mobile phone goes off in the middle of a heart-breaking Puccini aria, then it's an Italian event.

Apart for the occasional hitch (it can happen to everyone!), our Clubs, associations, Italian Cultural Institutes and even bars are the places where Italy takes its culture to be shared with the locals and it usually does it really well.

Art, music and food: these are the three main Italian things you can 'taste' abroad. Italians are warm, hold their traditions dear, and want to share them, and to show off a bit. They take abroad with them their love of good things and their passion for music: famously, our pop singers, even when they are not as successful in Italy as they used to be, stage wonderful, enthusiastic concerts in Canada, Russia or the UK. The Italian audience abroad is usually warm and well-behaved, and I have seen beautiful pop concerts in London – well organised and even starting on time!

These events happen more and more often. Capitals like London and New York, but also smaller towns like Liverpool and Edinburgh, schedule a lot of Italian–related festivals, exhibitions, concerts and parties. But these are not the only moments where Italy is observed abroad of course. Together with the Italian ex-pat and the Italian politician on official visit, the Italian on Holiday embodies and represents Italy all over the world. This is why it's worth looking at how Italians travel, how they manage to deal with airports, stations, timetables and generally the Art of Moving Around.

Firstly, as in many other situations, Italians on holiday don't go unnoticed. If in doubt, check out the sunglasses, the real fur coat, the expensive camera, the state-of-the-art mobile phone. These Italians make a certain impression when they travel. For the Italians, surely, holidays have become increasingly important in recent years. We spend a lot on travel and have become more adventurous.

Former Deputy Foreign Minister Danieli, during his recent London visit, told us journalists that expenses for rescuing Italians in dangerous parts of the world while on holiday are becoming an alarming part of the Ministry's budget.

Italians have changed a lot since the 1960s, when, thanks to the '*boom economico*', as it was called, they could afford one yearly beach holiday in their new Fiat. With more money in our pockets (well, at least until the Euro arrived) and more free time during the year, we have become a demanding lot who want to show off with their friends, often by going to exotic destinations or on adventure trips. In fact Italians are possibly the only nationality still sending postcards.

Sometimes we get into trouble: the image of the Daring Holidaymaker is starting to take its place next to the one of the Rich Traveller, the Sex God and the Glamorous Housewife, at least in world's imagination regarding Italians. Also, we are not what you would call 'organised' most of the time.

So, famine, disastrous weather conditions, unfortunate losses of suitcases, non-existent hotels in the desert, arrests for drug dealing mix-ups and, ultimately, the urgent need to be rescued from an unknown island in the Pacific by the Italian authorities have all appeared in the headlines in recent years. We do like improvising, but it might be better for most of us to avoid it when we plan our holidays.

Of course, English-speaking parts of the world remain among the favourite destinations for the Italians. In a capital like London, that welcomes millions of tourists, I am still amazed to see that very often I can recognise an Italian family visiting Trafalgar square, maybe from the enthusiasm

I can see in their eyes but there are other clues. You need to have *le physique du rôle*, of course. If you can afford a holiday to the UK, then you can also afford expensive gadgets and status symbols.

Mum carries an expensive designer bag, wears posh shoes and real fur. Dad usually wears a heavy leather coat, expecting all weather conditions. In fact, every Italian is convinced that the UK is cold, wet and miserable most of the year, so they only pack heavy jumpers, snow boots, long padded coats good for the frost and the ice they might find. Even in June. Well, you never know. Better safe than sorry.

The children have an Invicta backpack, a nice iPod and expensive mobile. In fact, even if there are no official statistics on this, I think Italian kids might beat any other country in the world for age of first mobile owned. It ranges from three to four-and-a-half, on average. They won't be able to form numbers, but they will learn to play the phone's games immediately.

Another distinctive character is the walk: Italians *passeggiano*, which broadly translates as strolling, but the exact meaning does not exist in English. It's a slow walk usually made arm in arm looking at the ground and chatting away. Monuments can wait. Of course, some Italians just walk with their heads in the air taking photos of everything, from the bus stop to the pretty plastic restaurant sign.

Italians in the UK usually complain about high prices here, so they stay in B&Bs but don't have the full English breakfast: how can you eat bacon and eggs at nine in the morning? They also think anything that sounds Italian must be Italian. For example: a group of Roman tourists at a bus stop looking at a number 24 bus, '*Guarda, questo va a Via Camden, ce l'abbiamo sulla cartina?*' (Look, this goes to Via Camden, do we have it on the map?), thinking that via must mean road, like in Italian.

When you look at us on holiday all over the world you might have contrasting feelings. You also realise that, generally, copying our sense of style is a good thing, but copying the tourists' sense of style does not always pay.

Fat men with dyed hair who wear black leather jackets and heavy gold chains showing through an open neck shirt, short plump women with tight leather miniskirts, fishnet stockings and high heels don't need to be copied.

But let's have a closer look at the three most common prototypes of Italian tourist abroad:

1. *Turista Pasticcione* (the Mr Bean-like tourist) – Leaves things behind. Doesn't have a clue about accommodation in the place he's going to. Has 'vaguely' booked a room but forgot to confirm. Sincerely hopes he's going to make it to the place. Improvises and *'si arrangia'* otherwise. Records everything on camera, Mr Bean style. Wishes he did not have to go but has promised his partner/mother/cousin/ so can't get out of it. Will usually be fine with a bit of luck.

2. *Turista Previdente* – has researched the destination carefully on the Internet. Has then chosen perfect accommodation, booked it, confirmed it, booked flight, car hire/transfer. Usually gets struck by bad weather, his suitcase gets stolen/lost/accidentally catches fire. Loves travelling, though, and usually chooses exotic destinations.

3. *Turista Pavone* – This person's motto is: It doesn't matter where you go, make sure you get noticed! It's a necessity for this kind of Italian tourist to have the latest designer glasses/ski gear/clothes/bag. They'll often choose *'settimana bianca'* (skiing week) where they can pretend not to be feeling too good, and so can sit on the veranda watching the others ski, while sipping cocktails and showing off equipment/clothes/beautiful hair/nice tan.

And here, again, I must quote my friend Martin Solly and his *Xenophobe's® Guide*:

'Cross-country skiing enjoyed a boom when skin-tight Lycra ski-suits were invented. It was worth braving the freezing cold and the physical agony for a couple of hours in order to be able to show off in the bar afterwards (and it might have been good for your health, too).'

These three examples of tourists are of course just a simplification. The Italians being travellers and poets, many more types can be seen trotting the globe. But one thing you have to keep in mind: the Italian traveller is welcome wherever he goes. Because, with a few exceptions, they like to spend money on holiday; more than in the gym. They like to take it easy and have comfort, even luxuries, wherever possible. There is no need to do much: a little stroll, a visit to the must-see places, then a nice dinner in the hotel and maybe a theatre or concert afterward. There is in fact another fool-proof way to recognise an Italian among other European tourists: the way they know how to take it easy and have fun without doing much. That's why people go on holiday, to rest, don't they?

When I interviewed Nico Tulini, 38, an engineer, I thought his comments on this subject were very good:

'Italians can relax without doing anything at all, when they travel. If you imagine German, Swiss and Italians on a resort, you can immediately sort out where they come from. The Germans and Swiss get up early and do all sorts of things, they run, swim, horse-ride. The Italians get up late, have breakfast, read the paper, talk about nothing with their friends. Their first thought is not what to do, but where to have lunch. The Italians are individualistic in their way of acting and thinking, but sociable in their leisure time. A central value to his life is food, for example. Take an average

German: he relates to society in his way of acting and thinking, and is individualistic in his leisure time. We are the other way round. And we can enjoy company like no other people.'

6. The Rules of Attraction

'Typically, [Italian women have] black flashy eyes, thick hair, full lips, curvaceous figures and a natural grace. This sort of image was one that provided foreigners with the pleasure of difference. Compared to the refined and artificial Frenchwoman, the remote and composed English rose and, later, the sporty and emancipated American, the vital and untamed Italian woman offered a promise of warmth and passion, a sense of full acceptance of her biological destiny, a strong link to place and a comforting refusal to encroach upon the prerogatives of men.'

– Stephen Gundle writing in his book Bellissima about the origins of the deep interest of Northern Europeans for Italian women.

IT WAS A BRIGHT, COLD DAY IN JANUARY 2008, AND A group of about seventy people met up in front of the Sainsbury Wing of the National Gallery, in Trafalgar Square. They were carrying posters and placards saying 'Save Siena', 'No to Siena Airport', 'Do not pave over Tuscany'. It was the last day of the magical National Gallery exhibition 'Renaissance Siena: Art for a City': the perfect occasion. I was invited, too and realised it was in fact a group of English young people who felt so passionate about Siena, having been there, often having spent all their summers there. They wanted to fight against the expansion of this small airport to save our countryside. *The Sunday Times* was there too and dedicated half a page to this demonstration the following day: it was perhaps a small event, but it was an amazing example of the love so many people have for Italy. It included children and families, fashion models and sons of nobles like Fred Lambdon, grandson of the late Earl of Durham, who had organised the demonstration. As he said to me in an interview for the Sienese paper *Corriere di Siena*, 'We want to keep Tuscany as it is, without industries or pollution, that is why we are fighting the project of an airport'. I wrote about this demonstration in the Tuscan papers, I sent a few pieces to them and to English websites about Italy. Because the interesting thing was also this strange, strong connection Italy and Britain seem always to have had. So many other countries also seem to be attracted to Italy and its beautiful landscape, people, food, culture: it is possibly one of the most loved places in the world.

The Mystique of Italy, and why the world is attracted to it is a subject my husband and friends often talk about. It's an intriguing factor, its charisma, and has that unusual characteristic of being hard to explain: a phenomenon that goes back centuries. Of course, it's a two-way thing: we Italians love many aspects of the English-speaking countries of the world: there are many couples, businesses, societies and websites that unite the Italians in their passion for places like the UK, Australia and the USA, and they're growing steadily.

Of course, if you ask them why they keep falling in love or starting businesses with each other, it's difficult to get an answer. In fact, if you ask these people why they chose each other, you get several different answers. And, all over the world, British-Italian societies, American-Italian societies, clubs and online communities are frequently being formed. Needless to say, the British, Americans, Australians and Canadians love our art, and of course our culture, food, wine and design. We Italians love American soaps, Australian serials and Hollywood films, we love London and New York and Sydney and Toronto because such large metropolises are fascinating to us: we don't have them in Italy. We also love Shakespeare, who loved Italy, the fish and chip shops and pubs, the elegance of some of Britain's villages and we absolutely adore Cornwall, Rosemunde Pilcher and red telephone boxes. We love America's highways, onion rings, Las Vegas, Elvis Presley, Marilyn Monroe, Bruce Springsteen, showgirls and TV shows with canned laughter.

But there must be more to it. I have asked people in the UK, USA and Canada, both English and Italian, to explain the attraction between our cultures.

The presence of many Italians abroad since the nineteenth century and earlier has of course encouraged the mutual love between Italian culture and the English-speaking world. But the reputation of Italians hasn't always been spotless: involvement with Mafia and crime, our controversial politics, but also the poor life that many of the Italian families led when they first arrived in the USA or in the UK must have been all somewhat negative factors in the eyes of the natives.

But the attraction was already there. 'There is interest and love for the Italians' – some have said to us – 'and the interest is mutual.' 'Love and hate are sometimes connected in the relationships that develop' – an American friend added – 'but certainly knowing the generosity and warmth of the Italians has been a key factor in this century-long love story!'

When people ask me why I love Britain and why I left sunny Tuscany for it, I haven't got a clear answer myself. Maybe it's quite natural to fall in love with the homeland of the person you love. But there is more to it than that. I have thought about it a great deal. After all, when I came to the UK I knew the language but that was about it. When I arrived at Stansted for the first time, one dark rainy December evening, to visit my future husband for a short holiday, I thought it was a dream: the road that took us to central London was great! All the small pointy houses in the rain, with no curtains drawn or shutters closed, so you could see everything inside! I thought it was odd, for a very private people like the English. In Italy we close our shutters as soon as dusk comes. Of course I loved the cars driving on the left, the emotions I felt while travelling through this unknown country on a winter's night, all the Christmas decorations, and then all the pulsating life of the capital embracing me in its warm glow.

Places like London, but also Scotland, Wales, Kent and the Northern parts of England, with their old cathedrals topped with Gothic spires are peculiar and interesting to us, they are *nordiche*: they remind us of old tales and mythical fairytale characters, and they hold a firm place in our imagination.

As for the people, I think we love to discover that there is more to them than their calm, sensible behaviour. The *flemma Britannica*, the poise and stiff upper lip, the way of approaching things with a quiet smile and a rational explantion for everything is like a challenge to us. So, we make a point of proving that eccentricity, craziness and passion are also part of the British soul. You just have to bring them out, and in Italy it's somehow easier. I have noticed that sometimes, when in contact with a more direct and spontaneous way of behaving, like we Italians have, the British – once they overcome the initial worry and scepticism – often manage to feel at ease and begin to express their inner originality in different ways. They can relax in Italy: I have seen many members of my English family changing and becoming more direct, warm and sensuous when they spend time in Italy. When Dame Edith Sitwell published *The English Eccentrics* in 1933 she may not have thought that the book would still be so frequently read nowadays. I think the idea of the English actually being irresponsible, unusual, unpredictable and a little bit crazy is the most fascinating glimpse into the English soul I have ever read – apart from, perhaps, *How to be a Brit* by George Mikes. His book is an exceptionally funny and still quite an accurate take on the British soul and the way it relates to us foreigners.

I believe that all these eccentricities and spirit come especially alive when the Italians and the British come together. Surely it's another reason why we like each other so much!

* * *

While Italians and Americans somehow have quite a lot in common – we are often both loud, excitable, warm and extroverted peoples – the British and the Italians don't have so many shared characteristics.

The British look for our sunny side, the unexpected, the passion and the flavours. We are fascinated by the genteel and sometimes reserved side of the British. We love the British monarchy, of course, Italy being a nation that never forgot its kings. In fact, it's incredible how much space is given in the Italian news to the British Royal Family. For us Queen Elizabeth and her entourage have always been a source of fascination, with all their humanity, faults and contradictions, but still with their fairytale aura.

The British love to criticise our irresponsible, sometimes unpredictable approach to sport, especially football, but give a lot of time to programmes like *Football Italiano* (with its pretty Italian co-presenter) and produces several magazines on the subject.

Britain's TV channels also run many shows on Mediterranean cuisine, buying a house in Tuscany, getting married in Umbria, starting a business in Italy, and so on.

But what do the people really think? When I posted a question on www.italiansoflondon.com about the love story between the British and the Italians, I received some good replies. Marta Lusini wrote: 'They often seem cold and organised, but they also have an eccentric side to them which we like. Where else will you find cheese rolling competitions or ferret racing?'

This eccentric, but cool side of the British character was also at the heart of the 1972 film *Fumo di Londra* by, and starring, the great comic actor Alberto Sordi. The character dreams of visiting London, which he considers the capital of style and fashion, and when he does, he realises he's about the only one still wearing a bowler hat and a *fumo di Londra* suit (*fumo di Londra*, or London Smoke, is a type of grey fabric).

As for other countries, I was interested in why the Americans and the Italians seem to be attracted to each other. I found many answers in a couple of friends who live in San Francisco, Jerry and Toby Levine. They just think that, although there is a lot to be said against the Italian politics and economy, Italy is a world leader when it comes to food and the arts: 'In no other country can you find such good food – apart from possibly China to take out – and the arts are so incredible, although there are too many tourists in towns like Venice and Rome, and not enough in other places. The love story between the US and Italy will never end because of all these reasons. And many Italians have always chosen the United States to live and work: we have many Italian families in San Francisco, and people love them'.

I also asked my husband's stepsister Harriet, who is Canadian, to explain what she thinks of the Italians and how she feels Canada perceives us. She told me that there are many big families of Italian origin, many of them lovely people, although a few of them are involved in crime. But the fact is, there, too, the Italians have a reputation for being warm, sunny, extrovert and funny, generous and extremely interesting in their mixture of improvisation and arts, exuberance and sense of family, friendliness and imagination. And the Italians seem to love the climate, although very cold, and the variety of Canada: that is why so many of them chose to live there.

At the same time, of course, many foreigners choose to live in Italy: increasingly, it's the British and Americans. They write books on our beauties and problems, on our picturesque but difficult country. New Italian businesses are formed often, and there is a number of Internet sites and events where our two cultures meet. As Beppe Severgnini usefully points out, the idyllic books on Italy are usually written by American women who often fall in love with our 'seasonal Eden', while the 'diaries of disappointment' are usually created by British men who think we are a 'disturbing country' with unreliable people and dodgy government. But the very high number of books on us as a country, the frequent articles in the international press about Italy and all the interest that there is in a mutual way of relating to each other, show how much this connection between Italy and the rest of the world keeps growing.

Part 2 - The Pleasures (and Pains) of Bel Paese

'Well, Italy is making the headlines again ... Possibly another sleaze story about football, you might think? No ... According to scientists at Leicester University, people stay healthier for longer, in Italy, compared with those in other European countries ... After all, with Italy and its politicians and its economy forever in dire straits, perhaps we deserve the chance to feel a little full of ourselves, and full of a little good advice too.'

– Guido Santevecchi, 'Living La dolce Vita', the Guardian, 4 July 2006

NOW THAT WE HAVE LOOKED AT THE IMAGE THAT Italy and the Italians export abroad, and the way they see themselves, it's time now to introduce what it actually means to live like an Italian. The food, art, sex, sport, politics, music, fashion and design of Italy tend to fill up the pages of the magazines as an example, and sometimes as a warning. But with all our faults and contradictions, we are still among the most copied populations in the world, mostly because we love life. And we know how to enjoy it.

Part two of our journey into Italy will include chapters on food and drink, fashion and sport, motoring and art, music and politics, focusing on the good rather than the bad.

It will also offer advice on how to eat well, as we do, on how to enjoy beauty and art, and on how to learn to be just slightly Italian in the way you look at things.

Sdrammatizzare is an art consisting of the opposite of melodrama, of taking the bad out of things and being able to see the good that can be achieved in how we go about our daily lives. We Italians believe there is a recipe for the good life even when things appear wrong, even when the taxman wants sixty per cent of your earnings or the government is falling apart, even when the traffic is awful and you have just received a fine for parking in a spot where you've never actually parked at all.

As Trevis Neighbor Ward and Monica Larner put it in their book *Living, Studying and Working in Italy*, Italy has found a proper place in which it exists between tradition and change, and, although separated into regions, into North and South, into progress and division, although plagued by bad governments and an awkward legal system, by debt, corruption and by a struggling economy, our lifestyle is still possibly the best in Europe, according to these scientists quoted by Santevecchi.

So, while Italy has allegedly been 'going wrong' in these recent years – in its politics, institutions and legal system, we have developed our passion for crafts into small business, our passion for food into a cuisine which is envied and loved by the world, our passion for design into production of cars, clothes and objets d'art that are truly successful. But mainly we have kept our optimism, being able to take the best from everyday routines and even from everyday troubles and contradictions.

And how did we do it? Ah, that's the point. Let me show you that you can live in a difficult but wonderful country and still be able to keep your hopes, figure, sense of humour and enterprise. Here's how to live like an Italian.

7. The Food and the Wine: How to Stay Fit and Healthy at the Table

'A good cook is like a sorceress who dispenses happiness'

– Elsa Schiaparelli

'The Italians are foodcentric people. Much of Italian life revolves around the growing, buying, preparing and, above all, eating of food. Whenever possible, meals are shared and eaten in company ... Italian enthusiasm knows no bounds when it comes to arranging a meal ...'

– Martin Solly, The Xenophobe's® Guide to the Italians

THE LARGE FLAT IN THE CENTRE OF FLORENCE WAS really breathtaking: the old pictures on the wall, the ceramics, the large windows overlooking the piazza flooded by the afternoon sunshine. Then Marinella came to the door to welcome us, smiling, with tiny steps on the old flowery carpet. '*Cocca*,' she said to my mother, '*se aspetti un pochino ti fo qualcosa per pranzo … Eh, cucinare è bello!*' Which translates as 'little chick, if you wait a bit I will cook you something for lunch … Cooking is good!'

Marinella was my mother's great aunt: and it wouldn't sound so amazing, really, if she wasn't one hundred years old at the time and still fully independent in her own flat. When we turned down her offer, she started to talk about her youth: she still remembered some of the recipes she cooked for her Signora, Violet Trefusis, who was a friend of Virginia Woolf and a wonderful writer in her own right. Violet lived in Florence for many years, and Marinella Lanini was her cook at the Villa dell'Ombrellina. She used to tell us stories from some of the wonderful parties she helped to prepare at the Villa when the English crème de la crème were coming to stay in Florence.

It's not by chance, I think, that she lived healthily until 102. Her brother, Lorenzo Lanini, also a cook, is now ninety-five, and cooking and eating well, together with a positive outlook, have been for both of them the keys to a long, happy life. Incidentally, both Marinella and Lorenzo refused, a couple of years ago, to spend their holidays in a convent with nuns while Lorenzo's daughter went on her own holiday … they simply stated that they would not stay for two weeks in a convent 'full of old people'.

Italy *is* the land of good food. I'll quite happily agree with that particular stereotype. This time it's all true. Our ingredients, recipes, flavours, produce and dishes are loved by people of every nationality and age. In Italy life expectancy is greater than in most countries and good food plays a huge part.

Tradition, passion, care and creativity are paramount in our kitchens: Italian food, with its centuries-old traditions, is possibly the best loved in the world. Cooks are respected and admired more than TV stars in Italy, which says a lot about a country where televisions are on and blaring most of the time.

* * *

I come from a family of landowners who gave more importance to olive-oil making than to literary studies, so I was regarded as slightly strange when I decided to go to university, the first to do so among my forty-five first cousins.

But I wanted to learn literature and journalism, without neglecting my peasant origins, so I continued living on the Tuscan farm with my parents and grandparents while driving to Siena University four days a week. This way I could enjoy both the country life and the cultural realities of a beautiful and ancient town, all its events, music, theatres, art and traditions. That way I could also keep in touch with friends and family in Siena and Tuscany.

Living in a country village where life was, and is, indeed marked by the seasons, by the different kinds of work in the fields and by rites that unite all the families for the grape harvest or the olive picking, I couldn't ignore the pleasures of cookery, and very early in life I became interested in learning the best dishes of our region. My grandmother Iva was from Montalcino, she loved the great wines there, and all the slow-cooked meats and old-fashioned soups. My mother Tosca was, like me, born on the farm we still own where everything was at hand: fresh vegetables, pulses, herbs and fruit to pick in our garden, wine in the cellar, extra-virgin olive oil just pressed, chickens and pigeons and ducks in the 'pollaio', wild mushrooms, chestnuts and game in the woods just behind the farm, wild salads growing on the green hills. Then there were my aunts, Mara, who lives in the same village, Lupompesi, and Giulia, my father's sister, living in Florence but born near Benevento.

These people, like *zio* Lorenzo and *zia* Marinella, are all excellent cooks and have taught me a lot of beautiful dishes. I now share them with my friends in London who love coming to dinner.

The incredible richness of all these influences, together with the luxurious gifts of our land were a sort of given for all of us at the time – only now that I have to go and shop for lettuce and tomatoes do I sometimes regret not being able to pick them in my fields. But I make up for it on frequent trips back to Tuscany.

As Donatella Cinelli Colombini, the renowned Montalcino winemaker and Siena councillor for tourism, often says, cookery is in our DNA. We breed the same pigs that were painted by Ambrogio Lorenzetti in his *Good Government* frescoes in the Siena Palazzo Pubblico in the Middle Ages. We eat cakes rich with pepper, candied fruit and honey, invented possibly in the thirteenth century. So cooking is a deeply ingrained part of each of us and we are very proud of it.

Learning to cook for us young girls of the village was a game, but we also grew up with a strong idea in mind: *'gli uomini si prendono per la gola'*, my grandmother used to say, which literally means: 'It's good to take men by their throat'. In a small country village, for my friends and me at the age of fourteen, the idea of getting married when we grew up was, of course, essential. But then in our later teens we naturally reconsidered and opted for university first, and a bit of fun before finding the 'right one'. Yes, because, as my grandmother used to say, 'Mr Right is out there and he will wait for you.' 'But what if there isn't a Mr Right for me?', I objected. My grandmother insisted: at one point, Mr Right would indeed come – and he would be hungry.

We learned to cook, for us, for our families, for prospective husbands and for friends, for the neighbours who came to pick the olives with us. Cooking and eating was for us, and still is, a pleasure made of good clean flavours and simple, fresh ingredients.

Growing up in Tuscany meant that the recipes we learned were healthy and simple; based on good olive oil and herbs, bread and homemade pasta, pulses, eggs and white meats, plus of course huge amounts of vegetables and fruit straight from our amazing gardens. What you find now in many Italian restaurants is of course derived from this tradition of flavours and creativity, although, especially in our restaurants abroad, there has been a lot of evolution on these themes, sometimes taking our cuisine beyond what it originally was.

The best Italian cookery, as Beppe Severgnini often reminds us, is simple and has no frills. He also writes of 'spontaneous gustatory proficiency that cuts across classes, age groups, income brackets, education and geographical boundaries', and in fact he also underlines how our 'honest, practical and working class' cookery has conquered the world – our country cookery is fantastic, too.

Of course new twists to old recipes are very fashionable and all, but the best dishes are those made of few simple, fresh, colourful ingredients like golden olive oil, purple aubergines, creamy garlic and, of course, good pasta. The best Italian soups are made with bread and vegetables, and possibly our most appreciated hors d'oeuvre is Bruschetta, slices of garlicky bread with fresh new olive oil still green and tingling on the tongue from the cold pressing.

In our modern restaurants, both in Italy and abroad, a dish like Bruschetta has become something often complicated by all sorts of toppings and accompaniments.

I'd like to give you a taste of some real Italian classic cookery, and so will give you a handful of recipes throughout this chapter, starting with:

BRUSCHETTA (pronounced: BroosKetta)
Serves 4

You will need:
A loaf of unsalted Tuscan bread (available from Italian delicatessen like Delizie d'Italia – see Appendix)
250 ml extremely good extra virgin olive oil
A wood fire (or a grill)
5 garlic cloves

Slice the bread into 1.5 cm thick slices and pass under a medium grill until golden on both sides. (In Italy, we sometimes put a grill rack on a wood fire and lay the bread on it, turning once). Peel the garlic cloves, cut in two, and when the bread comes out hot from the oven or grill, rub the garlic generously over one side of the bread. The aroma will be astonishing. Then pour gently quite a large amount of olive oil onto each slice and serve immediately. (You can, if you wish, add a sprinkle of salt, but this will somehow change the flavour of the olive oil: if the oil is good, it will have enough flavour as it is.)

This is how we taste the new olive oil straight from the olive press, it's the best way to judge if it's been a good year.

The secret of this recipe is in the ingredients. If you use a different type of bread or poor extra virgin olive oil, the dish loses its appeal, even its essence. But if you have the luck of getting cold-pressed pure extra-virgin oil in Italy from a small producer (like me!) or Frantoio (the oil-press centres usually sell olive oil), then you will taste the real Bruschetta.

And, purism aside, I cannot deny that laying a few slices of fresh, ripe tomato on the garlicky bread is good too: but then don't call it bruschetta, call it *pane al pomodoro*; a very popular snack in Italy among children, it's also good on bread that hasn't been grilled, as the soft slice will absorb the juices of the tomatoes and taste heavenly.

Italian cookery is all about ingredients, more than about skill. Once you have made a recipe, it will be easy to make it again and again, because many of our dishes are quite simple.

The richness of our land is of course the reason for the availability of such wonderful ingredients. Already in 1963, when the second edition of *Italian Food* by Elizabeth David was published, the author underlined the huge variety of ingredients available on Italian soil – a gift of nature that is the real secret of our best dishes. Our agriculture is rich in grains, fruit and pulses, and our woods produce amazing truffles and fantastic mushrooms from North to South. Our seas, being among the cleanest in the world, are stocked with excellent fish, hunting is still very popular in many regions, so game is another mainstay of Italian cuisine. Our regions, from Marche to Piemonte, Toscana to Emilia, have a great variety of cattle breeds, our pigs and sheep are renowned for their flavour and of course the sun makes our tomatoes the best, juiciest and reddest you can find. If you add to that lots of honey producers, our extra virgin oils that are light and tasty, our wonderful wines and spirits like grappa or Marsala, our cheeses from Gorgonzola and Pecorino to Parmesan and Mozzarella, the picture is complete. What more could one want?

* * *

In Italy we are still straightforward with food and we Italian women like spoiling our men and children with it. Even film stars like Loren or Cucinotta are not afraid of declaring how much their role as cook in their kitchens is still important even though they are VIPs. In fact, among people of all ages, cooking has always been a favourite way to relax and enjoy life, and a good excuse to throw parties and spend time together.

Everybody loves good food in Italy: it's not by chance that the Slow Food movement was born here – the antithesis of fast food, which has become such a dominant feature in people's eating habits in so many other countries. Slow food preaches the opposite of the idea of grabbing a burger or a sandwich for lunch, the principle being that eating slowly and carefully choosing your food is the key to good nutrition and ultimately to a good life.

Of course Italy has McDonalds and Burger King; people on their lunch breaks will grab a burger and fries in our cities and towns, but the culture of good food and wine is ultimately hugely important to us, and nobody would miss the lack of fast food chains in Italy if they disappeared overnight and were replaced with *trattorie*.

The *trattoria* idea itself is a winning one, and it represents the essence of our cuisine. A Roman *trattoria* is surely more interesting and exciting than a high-end restaurant, because it will offer you the typical recipes of Lazio, for example, the rice *supplì* and the wonderful meat dishes, just to mention a couple, and simple but aromatic *Vino dei castelli* to go with it. Every town and village offers its own family-run *trattoria* or *osteria*, and it's not rare to find authentic jewels of cookery in the smallest places.

For example, in my area there are quite a few nice, big restaurants, but the only two that are known all over Tuscany and which appear in the travel guides are Pizzeria dell'Arco in Murlo, which makes the best pizza in the Siena province, and Osteria da Brunero, in a tiny place called La Befa, where you can get the best wild boar dishes in the world.

In this and other trattorias, you can discover the secret of real Italian pasta dishes and sauces, for example. Which triggers 'that old question': How *is it that Italians can eat a lot and don't get fat*? This can be answered in many ways, but mainly with one little secret: use as many complex carbohydrates as you like, but only very few fats. Eat pasta, but with the right seasoning.

This is the idea behind our sauce recipes: tomato-based sauces are the ones we use with most frequency, and they are the lower-fat ones, since they only use a spoon of olive oil and nothing else in the way of fats. Even if you look at our most famous sauces like Arrabbiata or Napoletana, tomatoes are the main ingredient, together with garlic or onion, and fresh herbs, so they won't make you fat! There is one main sauce that is loved all over Italy: the basic tomato sauce for pasta, the easiest, quickest and possibly best, especially if you use good chopped tomatoes or *passata*. In Italy, especially in the countryside, the chopped tomatoes are often fresh in the summer, but also in many places *passata* is still made at home, in large quantities, and can be kept all year in glass bottles. The *passata*-making (in some areas we call it *conserva di pomodoro*) is another rite that has been handed down from one generation to the next, since about the fourteenth century. In Tuscany, in Central and South Italy, in August, you can often find whole families engaged in the production of this ingredient: the small children pick huge amounts of tomatoes, the mothers and grandmothers peel and mash them and make them into *passata*, then the men bottle the beautiful mixture (which can be plain or mixed with herbs and chilli) and boil it in large pans over an open air fire before storing it in the cellar.

If you are in Italy on holiday and you happen to have friends or neighbours who store some of these bottles in their pantry, well, do anything you can to get one as a present: you won't find anything like this in the shops. If you do get your hands on some good *passata*, try this recipe, it's my mother Tosca's (but also common in some variation or other in many households):

SALSA DI POMODORO PER LA PASTA
(basic tomato pasta sauce)
Serves 2

You will need:
One tablespoon of good olive oil
One clove of garlic
One small red onion
Salt and pepper
1 tin of chopped tomatoes (or half a bottle of
    homemade Passata di pomodoro)
1 teaspoon of oregano

Pour the oil into a pan and slice the garlic, add the onion cut thinly into half-moon slices, season with salt and pepper, then fry over medium heat. The garlic and onion must cook until they become golden, otherwise they won't develop their flavours fully. At this point, lower the heat and cook the sauce for 12–15 minutes (the time to cook and drain the pasta is usually enough, so if you start the sauce before boiling the water, and then cook it while the pasta is cooking, it will be enough). Turn off the heat and add the oregano. Pour the sauce over hot pasta cooked *al dente* and serve.

* * *

All these recipes are taught from one generation to the next, but of course there are a few 'codes' of Italian cookery, books that are essential to understanding our basic methods and techniques as well as the key recipes of our cuisine. The Bible of Italian cookery is often considered to be the one published in 1891 by Pellegrino Artusi, *La scienza della cucina e l'arte di mangiare bene*, in which Artusi practically 'invented' the idea of Italian cookery in a young Italy. He codified recipes like *gnocchi* and *pasta al pomodoro*, so they became, with Artusi, for the first time, Italian dishes.

It wasn't just the cookery: his book, which he published at his own expense after many rejections from publishers, was promulgating a certain idea of Italy as a gastronomic land of delights, but also a land united in its taste for good, freshly prepared dishes to be served in the ways we do even now, from *antipasto* to *dolce*.

So his *crostini di fegatini di pollo*, a delicious recipe from Tuscany, his pasta dishes, meat courses and vegetables were an authentic way to discover our culinary traditions and make them available to everybody, in every region, from North to South.

The *crostini*, for example, would deserve a chapter of its own: smooth pastes prepared with vegetables and meat mixed with natural flavours and sauces like mayonnaise, to produce lovely creamy spreads served in the form of small *canapès* are our most famous *antipasti*. But Artusi also catalogued dishes like the world-famous *zabaione*, and included Mediterranean recipes like couscous.

Those publishers must have regretted not accepting Artusi's book, because within only a few years it was reprinted many times. All through the twentieth century it constituted the Bible of every kitchen and in 2005 it was relaunched in a modern edition. But Pellegrino Artusi wasn't the first to decide that cookery was a good topic to write about: a long time before him, somebody else decided to present a book on Italian cuisine to the nation. In fact, historians think that the first cookery book ever published was Italian: it's entitled *De Honesta Voluptate*, a collection of nine books by Bartolomeo Platina, published in 1473! The book included advice on food hygiene, on diet, food preparation, and many chapters on fruit, vegetables, meats and game, fruits of the earth like mushrooms and truffles – an authentic treasure for those in love with our cookery.

The most 'modern' cookery book that was printed in Italy was, according to some, that of Bartolomeo Scappi, who worked for cardinals, popes and noble families all over Italy in the sixteenth century. 'The Mrs Beeton of the time', as Antonio Carluccio described him in a recent BBC2 programme all about Scappi, this writer and cook was a real celebrity and created dishes with a lot of spices and sugar, both very expensive at the time, which are not really to our modern taste today.

Some of his ideas, though, are still very much a part of our modern cookery: his love for mushrooms and wild herbs, vegetables, pork dishes, pasta like tortellini (already quoted in Scappi's book), risotto, along with our tendency to cook meat with wine and so on. What's most important about him, though, in my opinion (and in Carluccio's), is what he wrote about the direct link between good food and joy of life. His book is most of all a treaty on how the Italians of the time (rich Italians of course, as the poor didn't have access to most ingredients), found in food one of the most important keys to enjoying life. Somehow, Bartolomeo Scappi's book, containing recipes for Giulio III and Gregory XIII and for Venetian nobles Pietro Bembo and Andrea Cornaro, is the symbol of a tradition which goes back many, many centuries.

In fact, if you think of our regional cookery, it's interesting to point out how much Central Italian cookery is linked not only to Medieval and Renaissance cookery, but even to Etruscan traditions. This is, after all, Etruscan land: they landed in central Italy between the ninth and eighth centuries BC, possibly from Turkey, and settled there, greatly influencing life and culture here. From the findings in tombs and from frescoes, we have been able to assess the taste in food and wine of our ancestors. The Etruscans, who founded many of our towns in Tuscany and Lazio, had an enormous passion for eating, drinking, dancing and partying. We know that they used to make something similar to wine, but without the alcoholic process, that they used to eat stewed meat, dried fruit, honey-flavoured sweets and had a penchant for sweet and sour dishes.

In the last ten years, in fact, my village, Murlo, has been the centre of attention for geneticists researching the origins of the Etruscans: after comparing the DNA of Etruscan remains to the DNA of some Etruscan towns in Central Italy, that of the people of Murlo has been found to be the closest to the Etruscans'. The isolation of the village seems to have made it possible for the people's genetic strain to remain very close to that of their ancestors. There was a huge interest around these studies and even very recently the *New York Times** has reinforced this theory: so Murlo has been declared the land of the last Etruscans.

* * *

At the end of the 1990s, some gastronomers in Murlo decided to try and recreate an Etruscan banquet, which proved to be

*Nicholas Wade, DNA boosts Herodotus, account of Etruscans as Migrants to Italy , New York Times, 3 April 2007

very successful. The first Saturday of September, in the warm evening, the small wonderful village is illuminated by lanterns and flooded with music; here, a lucky group of guests eat and drink while watching dancing girls in antique costumes, to relive those atmospheric moments that were scuplted on the decoration of an ancient palace found near the hill of Murlo, in Poggio Civitate. (See architecture chapter.)

The Etruscan Banquet is a beautiful occasion, one of many that happen in Tuscany for different reasons. The night before the *Palio*, for example, in each *contrada* hundreds of people sit in the Sienese squares to eat fantastic grilled meats and pastas and breads, just as a way to share the emotions that run high before the horse race.

Here, you will find that the old and the very young, the teenagers and the couples, the middle-aged and the over-nineties sit together and have fun. Alcohol is not really an issue at these parties. We don't have pubs that exclude children, we don't have off-licences with strict opening hours (in fact we don't have off-licences at all). Children get used to small quantities of wine from around the age of 6 or 7, and they don't see wine as a forbidden pleasure.

I agree again with Severgnini here, when he writes that we educate children sensibly about drinking: we feel it's a duty within a family to let the children try a bit of alcohol now and then, so they don't see it as a rebellious thing to do: in Italy there is no legal minimum age limit for drinking, but very few teenagers get drunk.

So we party, eat and drink merrily like the Medicis used to do, like the peasants also, in their own simple way, used to do … at least once a month. At these tables, though, only a very, very small minority of these guests are overweight, and as you get closer, you'll realise that they're not Italian.

* * *

Keeping it simple but also rich and interesting is a must for our dishes. Our best recipes indeed are the simplest ones. We don't like spending a whole day in the kitchen – a couple of hours will do, as we like good presentation, but mainly we like strong flavours and easy recipes, pasta dishes made with tomatoes, chilli, capers, herbs and olives called *pasta alla puttanesca* (the whore's pasta). A rich, colourful dish with unique flavours. You can easily imagine Monica Bellucci or Claudia Cardinale cooking these dishes and serving them to the table wearing a low-cut dark red velvet dress, can't you? Yes, because, by the way, we don't like slaving over a hot stove wearing slippers and a loose T-shirt, thank you very much. Better to wear a miniskirt while making your pizza (much more inspiring for your man anyway!).

We love pasta and bread, fish and vegetables, grilled meats and cheese and wine. But we do believe in self-control, as I will explain later. We have mastered the art of keeping in shape whilst eating quite a lot. But why is it that the world thinks the Italians eat too much but in other countries people get much fatter than us, especially considering that now the so-called 'Mediterranean Diet' has been adopted by many other cultures, too? There are reasons!

For example, it seems that just less than a half of the people who replied to a recent British survey stated that their favourite food is Italian. And only three years ago the BBC broadcast the results of another survey about the British favourite dish: it was Spaghetti Bolognese, followed by curry in second place. So it's clear that Italian food appeals to everybody, especially the traditional dishes of our land. It's also important to understand that in Italy we have been consistently fighting against fashions like 'no carbohydrate diets' and still keeping our shapely figures by eating frankly quite a lot – often three course meals – and very often with a lot of grain-based food. Scientists of course now know that the complex carbohydrates of pasta and rice are far better than those found in cakes and pastries with lots of butter. But we also like our desserts, our creamy sauces and red meats. How do we keep in good shape in spite of this? And how is it that we consume quite a lot of fats and proteins as well as carbohydrates but remain among the skinniest populations in Europe?

It's important to remember, too, that we are not a country of gym-goers. We prefer passive sports, like watching football on TV and reading *La Gazzetta dello Sport* (the best-selling daily in Italy for many years now). And generally we much prefer burning calories in the bedroom.

I think the secret, though, is in three elements: knowing where to stop with the alcoholic drinks, not snacking on high-fat treats like crisps, and keeping an eye on portions.

The first and second elements go together. In fact, if you start drinking beer at six o'clock and fill up on crisps and nuts, by the time you are at dinner already you will have consumed a huge number of calories.

Our *aperitivi*, as ItaliansOfLondon group will tell you, are often a simple glass of wine or non-alcoholic drinks, served maybe with a good slice of *bruschetta*, or perhaps *grissini* and a slice of Parma ham. Crisps, pretzels or salted nuts are not our idea of snacks; we wouldn't dream of eating them with a glass of wine, which instead goes well with a *crostino* (canapé with smoked salmon or tuna sauce) or with a salami slice. We might spend an hour just preparing *crostini* for a dinner, baking tiny slices of bread with chopped cherry tomatoes, herbs and olive oil on top. Because, when we do have the time, we like to take care over preparing delicious food for guests. There's a cult of food in Italy that is comparable with our obsession for beauty and style.

As for portion sizes, let's compare for a moment what is served in a restaurant or pub in Britain to what you'll get in an Italian restaurant: now, it's frequent to find pasta dishes in restaurants, almost any restaurant in the UK, as well as many pubs. If you order a portion of Spaghetti Bolognese more often than not they will bring you a plate the size of a ping-pong table filled with mountains of overcooked pasta floating in a greasy meat sauce. The same thing sometimes happens in some of my non-Italian friends' homes: years ago, when we would be invited, knowing our love for pasta, our friends would try to cook it for us. After my merciless complaints, now we have found a compromise: they buy the pasta, I cook it! As my lovely Scottish sister-in-law knows very well, when we go to stay I am likely to take over her kitchen once a day to cook *penne carbonara* or even spaghetti with tomato sauce, which everybody enjoys. But I serve it in small portions, as nobody wants to miss out on the lovely other courses she cooks.

Basically, because our meals are composed of an *hors-d'oeuvre* or *antipasto*, a pasta dish or risotto, and a second course with side vegetables and sometimes a dessert, we need to keep our portions small. This is good for the health but also keeps things varied and interesting. Filling up on pasta is not what people want, contrary to some clichés.

Going back for a moment to Spaghetti Bolognese, I'm going to give you the real recipe, as the variations we see in restaurants and homes all over the world can contain anything from bacon to red and green peppers. Here is the proper recipe from Bologna, which in fact we call:

RAGÙ ALLA BOLOGNESE
Serves 4

You will need:
3 tablespoons of olive oil
50 grams of pancetta cubes
2 celery sticks
2 carrots
1 small red onion
250 grams of minced beef
half a glass white wine
400 ml of tomato *passata* or chopped tomatoes
salt and pepper

In a deep casserole, warm the olive oil with the pancetta cubes and cook it gently until transparent, then add the chopped vegetables. Cook over a medium heat for 5 minutes, then add the beef and fry for a further 7 minutes before adding the wine. When the wine has evaporated, add the tomatoes or *passata* and cook very slowly for about 1 hour. Add salt and pepper and serve the sauce on pasta cooked *al dente*.

A perfect way to serve this sauce is with homemade tagliatelle. Homemade pasta is easy to make (the dough simply consists of strong flour and egg - one egg per 100 grams of flour). But the secret to making it is all in the hands and elbows, and in the right rolling pin! My grandmother's rolling pin is a monument in our Tuscan kitchen: it consists of a 5cm-thick piece of wood, it's possibly over a metre long, and for years it made the most amazing *pappardelle*, *tagliolini* and *tagliatelle* of all sizes. I remember our homemade pasta for Sunday lunch: a wonderful bowl of golden ribbons dressed with juicy, shiny *ragù*, hare or wild boar sauce, and sprinkled with good freshly-grated parmesan cheese. Her pasta was a legend: she would cut it expertly and then keep it for a few hours to dry under white canvas cloths. When it was perfect for cooking, she would just drop it in hot salted water for only 2 or 3 minutes, depending on its thickness. A real feast.

As much as I loved my grandmother's *tagliatelle*, I should say that the recipe I quote here is by somebody else. Benedetta Sgroi is a wonderful cook who owns a restaurant in Arezzo. Now that she's in London, though, she has decided to do a wonderful thing: make real Italian homemade pasta 'live' at Brick Lane Market. So it's not hard to try her *tagliatelle* – at her stall called *Ciao Bella*: just go there on Sunday from 10am to 7pm and you will see with your own eyes how to make pasta and try some of Benedetta's wonderful food.

BENEDETTA'S TAGLIATELLE
Serves 8

You will need:
8 eggs
1 kilogram of flour
A pinch of salt

Basically, it's all about the dough. It has to be elastic, quite firm but still supple, and it has to be worked for at least 10 minutes before being rolled into a thin layer and then it can be rolled and cut into the shape you want. Of course, if you are making *lasagna*, you will have to cut it according to the shape of your oven dish, if you are making *tagliatelle*, then the strips should measure about one centimetre, but for *fettuccine* they should be half centimetre, and so on. Of course if you feel especially creative, then you can try pasta bows: long rectangles three centimetres by four, to be pinched in the middle to give small bows. Cook them in boiling salted water for no longer than 3 minutes.

All this pasta is wonderful with *ragù* and parmesan cheese on top, but you can also try it simply with good extra virgin olive oil, freshly grated parmesan and black pepper, or with a creamy sauce like porcini mushrooms sautéed with garlic and cooked in cream, pancetta cubes fried with courgettes and finished with cream and pepper, and so on. The possibilities are endless.

If you do go for *ragù*, it will be an absolute treat: we used to have *tagliatelle* with *ragù* every Sunday lunch. The *Ragù alla Bolognese* recipe in fact comes from Emilia Romagna but has been known all over Italy for a long time. Some other recipes of regional cookery have remained localised and it's only possible to try them in their particular areas of origin.

When Elizabeth David arrived to Italy the first time, in the 1950s, she noted how much regional cookery was important in Italy. She very intelligently noticed that the term 'Italian cookery' doesn't mean much to lots of Italians, as Florentine cooking, Venetian cooking, or dishes from the other towns of Italy are how we really categorise our cuisine. And she also added: that, while almost every Italian restaurant serves a dish called *tagliatelle Bolognese*, there is one way to try the real *ragù alla Bolognese*: by going to Bologna or to Emilia Romagna.

This is still true fifty years on. There are many myths about Italian cookery, and food writers like Claudia Roden have in fact preceded the new vogue for regional Italian restaurants appearing in every part of the world. Now that many capitals have Sardinian restaurants and Tuscan restaurants, Roman *pizzerie* and Milanese *trattorie*, a book like 'The Food of Italy' by Roden is precious, and follows David's suggestion of regionality in cooking.

Though it's best to go to Milan to taste *Risotto Milanese* and to Parma to try the best *tortellini*, thank God and the EU, Italian products can now be found almost anywhere. A*maretti*, Parma ham or *pecorino di Pienza* can be bought in most parts of Europe. I have found them in Prague and in Budapest, in the Algarve and in Inverness. Hurrah for globalisation. And for tradition, which, at least in the Italian kitchen, still means a lot.

Two other products that travel a lot, in many versions, all over the world, are *minestrone* and *risotto*. Italy is of course famed for its first courses and, together with pasta, this marvellous soup made of vegetables and the creamy rice cooked in many different ways are among the best-known creations of our cuisine.

Unfortunately, sometimes minestrone comes in cans and risotto in pouches. But I have got a fool-proof way to make both these dishes by following my mother Tosca's recipes. She, like me, loves first courses, and, together with cannellini bean soup and *ribollita*, her favourites include a brilliant minestrone and a perfect, creamy porcini mushroom risotto. Here are her recipes:

MINESTRONE DI TOSCA
Serves 4

You will need:
3 tablespoons of good olive oil
1 medium red onion
2 medium potatoes
1 medium courgette
A handful of green beans
2 carrots
3 cabbage leaves
2 celery sticks
4 basil leaves

2 small ripe tomatoes
300 grams of tubetti pasta (De Cecco is her
favourite pasta)
Some extra virgin olive oil to pour on top

Cut all the vegetables into cubes. Heat the olive oil in a deep pan and add the onion, fry for a couple of minutes, then add the rest of the vegetables. Add plenty of water, up to the middle of the pan (at this stage, my mum looks in the fridge to find an old crust of Parmesan cheese. If it's there, she drops it with the vegetables because 'it gives a creamy twist to the soup', she says.

Boil the soup for about 10 minutes, then add salt and pepper and the pasta. Cook the pasta for a minute less than it says on the packet, as it will go on cooking when you turn the soup off. Serve hot with some extra-virgin olive oil poured on the top.

RISOTTO AI PORCINI
Serves 4

You will need:
Three tablespoons of good olive oil
1 knob of unsalted butter
1 small red onion
1 large handful of dried porcini mushrooms
Some good chicken stock (or stock made with a cube)
Salt and pepper
250 grams risotto rice (Arborio)
1 extra knob of unsalted butter to add at the end

As I was saying before, we serve our first courses in small amounts, so we can enjoy the rest of the meal without getting too full, so this makes plenty of risotto as a starter. First, soak the porcini mushrooms in warm water for at least 15 minutes. Reserve the soaking juice. Chop the red onion and fry it in the oil and butter in a medium size pan for about 5 minutes. Add the rice and let it become coated in the oil and onion juices for at least three minutes, always stirring. Then add the porcini water and mix well. Add some stock to cover the rice and simmer for 5 minutes, stirring all the time. At this point add the chopped porcini mushrooms and mix well. Add more stock and cook the rice for about 12 more minutes on a low heat, while stirring often. Take off the heat, stir in the knob of butter and serve hot.

If you are lucky enough to go to Italy during mushroom season, around September-October (but also springtime, depending on the weather), and you can buy some to take home, or find some in the woods, then make this dish using fresh Porcini. Nothing compares to the flavour of this amazing gift of nature! Italian restaurants offer it all year round: don't forget to try it!

Our second courses are not as well-known as our first courses. We have wonderful salami and charcuterie, and of course the celebrated *Fiorentina* steak, a 500 gram T-bone steak cooked on an open fire, and our game dishes are favourites in Italian restaurants but these are best tried in Italy, in just the right places. For game, central Italy is again the best area to try, and in Florence you will have to try the steak. Its popularity suffered somewhat during the time of Mad Cow disease, but in time it returned to being a favourite in Tuscany. Famously, Dario Cecchini, the well-known country chef from Panzano, Siena, held a month of celebrations when beef was declared safe to eat again: meat lovers remember those times with warm delight!

Some years ago, when my husband was travelling on a

plane from London to Florence, he met a doctor on the flight. He was talking about working in London and other things, and then he said, dreamily: '*Ma per prima cosa quando arrivo mi faccio una bella Fiorentina!*' ('... but first thing when we land, I am getting myself a beautiful Florentine!') Rob couldn't believe this man was being so open with him: he thought the doctor meant a Florentine girl, not being familiar with the famous T-bone steak!

Italy is a country of meat-eaters, of course: our Parma hams and spicy sausages are famous everywhere. Large dishes of *bresaola* seasoned with lemon and pepper, or chopped rocket, are a relatively new way of serving sliced cold meats, but our tradition leans towards the famous '*grigliate*', that smell that's so wonderful on the long warm evenings. We sit under the stars and we cook huge amounts of pork, beef, lamb, sausages, ribs and all sorts of meat and fish on our long summer nights: it is so beautiful to eat these dishes in good company and with fresh salad from the garden, slices of Tuscan bread, good glasses of our wine and a good laugh and a joke from time to time! This, for me, is the taste of Italian friendship!

When I was little I was very skinny and somehow people were convinced I must not eat very much to be as thin as that. It was good: I got continuous small treats like raw eggs straight from our chicken's nests accompanied by a sip of red wine from the cellar, rice chocolates from my grandfather who bought them for me in the nearby village Vescovado (Lupompesi has never had shops) as well as the most wonderful meat from our butcher. To be eaten raw in the best *carpaccio* I have ever tasted. The thin, pink, fragrant, amazingly fresh slices of meat would be lying on a small coloured ceramic plate and seasoned just for me to have after the pasta or soup.

Here is how my grandmother Iva used to make it for us:

THE BEST CARPACCIO IN THE WHOLE UNIVERSE
Serves 2

You will need:
6 slices of beef fillet, cut really thinly (ideally from
Vescovado's butcher Romano Muzzi!)
1 lemon
Three tablespoons of excellent home-made extra-virgin
olive oil
A few leaves of fresh rocket
Salt and freshly milled black pepper

Lay three slices of beef on each plate, season with salt and
pepper, then squeeze half the lemon onto the meat and wait
a couple of minutes, then chop the rocket really thinly and
season with the olive oil. Leave to rest for 5 minutes then
serve.

Now, no dish is complete without a good vegetable side
dish – *contorno* – and a dessert at the end. Our vegetable
dishes are usually simple and colourful: perhaps, together
with deep-fried artichokes and *melanzane alla parmigiana*, the
most famous one of all is *peperonata*, the pepper stew that is
famous for its incredible flavour and its beautiful mix of
colours. I make it following the recipe of my grandmother Iva:

PEPERONATA
Serves 4

You will need:
2 yellow peppers
2 red peppers

2 green peppers
3 tablespoons of extra virgin olive oil
1 large red onion
2 large ripe tomatoes
2 tablespoons of red wine vinegar
Half a glass of water
Salt and pepper

Heat the olive oil in a large frying pan. Add the roughly chopped onion and fry it for 4–5 minutes. While it cooks, cut the peppers in two, take the stalks, seeds and the core out and cut them into large strips. Add to the pan and mix well, then fry for about 10 minutes until they become soft. Add the water and vinegar, salt and pepper and simmer over a low heat for at least 40 minutes. Add more water if required, stir well quite often as the peppers tend to stick to the pan. Serve hot or warm.

I am not a great one for desserts. I don't much like sweet things so I don't really go for cakes, but I like a good creamy dessert. The most famous one is possibly *tiramisù*, which you can find in supermarkets all over the world now. But how do you make the Best *tiramisù* Ever? I have asked my aunt Giulia, my father's sister, who cooks wonderful food and whose *tiramisù* is possibly famous in the whole province of Florence, where she lives.

What makes it different and absolutely perfect is her unique twist: small chunks of dark chocolate added to the mascarpone cream, you don't beat that easily! The other important thing is the fresh eggs: being in the countryside, she has fresh eggs every day so she can make this dessert the way it should be made. Supermarket eggs are not ideal, but if they are fresh and free range they can still be used. Zia Giulia has always had a large family, and in addition to that she loves cooking for her friends and relatives, so the portions are generous!

ZIA GIULIA'S TIRAMISU
Makes a large bowl of tiramisu – serves at least 6-8

You will need:
3 whole eggs, separated
2 egg yolks
5 tablespoons of sugar
500 grams of mascarpone cheese
1 packet of *savoiardi* (sponge finger) biscuits
60 grams of dark cooking chocolate, cut into small pieces
Cocoa powder
Some black espresso coffee

Mix the egg yolks with the sugar until they become fluffy and pale yellow. Add the mascarpone cheese and work to a smooth cream. Whip the egg whites until stiff, add them to the mascarpone and egg cream and mix very delicately. Add the dark chocolate to this mixture. Using a rectangular glass or ceramic dish, make a layer with the sponge biscuits and soak with some espresso coffee. Add a thick layer of the mixture – around 3cm thick – and arrange one more layer of biscuits and coffee on top, finish up with the remaining mixture and sprinkle the top with the cocoa powder. Cool in the fridge before serving.

* * *

Now, what wine do you serve with an Italian meal? Obviously, with Italy being the sixth largest producer of wine in the world, this is also a very important side of our cookery – high quality wine that comes from our hills. Everywhere in

Italy you will find evenings devoted to food and wine, for different occasions. Street parties and fêtes are common in our villages and towns. A patron saint's day, a first communion, a fair or *sagra* (something usually dedicated to a special fruit or produce like truffles, chestnuts, game etc) are celebrated nearly every weekend in all corners of Italy.

None of Italy's regions are short of good wine. And, if only a handful are really universally known, let me say that the quality of our wines is certainly exceptional.

A beginner Italian student of mine, from London, laughed when I asked her if she already knew the Italian words for some colours. 'Yes, of course, I know *rosso* and *bianco* and *rose* … I learned them to know how to buy wine!'

Deciding which are the best wines in Italy is possibly as hard as saying which are our best dishes. But it's worth mentioning that, as well as the most known wines like Chianti or Brunello, Lambrusco or Valpolicella, there is a real wealth of white, red and dessert wines that needs to be discovered. Southern wines, for example, from Cirò di Calabria (the direct successor of that red wine given to the Olympics athletes competing in Calabria when the Greeks were here) to Solopaca, from Locorotondo of Apulia to Aglianico of Campania, the South really is a great place for tasting a good drop. These wines go well with the rich, aromatic cuisine of these regions.

Picture yourself on the fantastic coasts of Apulia, sipping maybe a Torre Quarto with some home-made *orecchiette*, looking at the 'wine-dark sea' as described by Homer: it does happen, and it's not just something for tourists. It's for everybody who enjoys life. There, only the strong, powerful flavours of wine and pasta will do. The red wine from the South is like an ancient song from many centuries ago: essential to recreate the dream of a lost land. The richness of the aromas in the air and the warm night lit with stars will do the rest, trust me.

Good wine, good food, good company, friendship, sex and laughter: I would say that these are most of the ingredients essential to living like an Italian, and for being healthier than our French, German or Spanish cousins.

As the press has underlined even recently, in Europe Italians are doing pretty well healthwise too. Is there a recipe for this? Undoubtedly, the quality of the ingredients, the tendency to eat properly, the avoiding of snacks, a different idea of socialising (we don't think you need to get drunk to have fun) and a steady eye on portions all contribute to a better lifestyle.

I would add one more thing though: this obsession of eating early in the evening, not having carbohydrates after a certain time etc, all sounds like nonsense to us.

On our long, balmy summer evenings it's natural to want to eat later, and even in the winter we like eating at a later time compared to most countries.

Our shops don't shut until eight o'clock in the evening, and there are things to do in the evenings before dinner. This is the time for the *passeggiata*, for a little chat or a Crodino drunk in the piazza watching the people and the Vespas go by.

Dinner at six o'clock sounds crazy to us. And it feels like a waste of time. So we won't usually sit at the table until eight at least. Possibly with family or friends, with our kids (who don't go to bed at seven and not even at nine very often).

Sitting in front of the TV by ourselves at six-thirty eating a huge, comforting plate of chips and a burger is not our idea of dinner, you see. Daily life in Italy is mostly just organised differently. So if we go to bed at eleven after a dinner eaten at nine we won't need a hot chocolate with cream or a large chocolate bar because we are hungry again.

If we go to a concert or show after dinner (concerts in Italy start at nine-thirty), we might just indulge in a *spaghettata di mezzanotte* or midnight spaghetti on our return.

This means you won't get up starving the next day, but also you will feel more relaxed after such an evening. And no, you don't need to open another bottle of wine; a chat with the family or with friends is much more important to us.

Life in the towns of course now has been changing hugely in Italy as well, but the bar culture in Milan or Rome or Florence sort of replaces the family idea of dinner. So, if we do have to have dinner by ourselves, we might just go to the bar for an espresso afterwards, for a chat and a laugh. Again, the 'togetherness' is part of this ritual.

Maybe we are just scared of solitude, or maybe it is just a different culture: but the figures show that people tend to be happier, more trim and socially more active in Italy – and the care we take over preparing and enjoying our food is central to our well-being and happiness.

8. Beauty And the Arts: Beauty is Everywhere in Italy – How to Deal with It

'The Creator made Italy from designs by Michelangelo'

– Mark Twain, 1835-1910

'The question of (female) beauty is so primordial an aspect of Italian culture, so diffuse and embedded in the national psyche, that it scarcely occurs to many Italians that it is a distinctive feature of their culture...'

– Stephen Gundle, *Bellissima*

MANY PHILOSOPHERS, WRITERS, ARTISTS AND thinkers have tried to define the special connection between Italy and beauty. The natural beauty of the land and the presence of beautiful people living on it represent a strong attraction for the millions of visitors who come here every year: but how best to describe the unique relationship that the Italians have with the beauty of their land itself?

It's said that sixty per cent of the world's fine art can be found in Italy and we are extremely lucky to possess so many masterpieces by some of the greatest artists in the world. Sixty-one Unesco World Heritage sites are located in Italy and the country has an amazing historical past.

The Renaissance was a hugely important period in Italy and some of the biggest scientists and artists of that time were born in our country, while the Middle Ages also had a huge impact on our territory, shaping the look of many of our towns. Our country has been proverbially kissed by the Gods: the climate, the variety of our landscape, the most beautiful seas, mountains and hills, magnificent islands and towns and incredible sites, from prehistory to modern times, have made Italy a unique and exciting place. Not many countries in the world can boast as many beautiful churches and villages: in Italy even the tiniest place often has a beautiful church, and it's not uncommon to find that great artists have produced their works for small churches or palaces.

Last summer my family and I stayed on the Monte Amiata, between Grosseto and Siena, and we realised that in Santa Fiora's church there was a beautiful Luca dalla Robbia: Asciano, and a small village south of Siena has a fantastic altar piece which was the main feature of the Renaissance Siena exhibition at the National Gallery in 2007.

Of course, it's a well-known fact that the Italians have a very strong sense of beauty. It's perhaps a genetic thing: after all, our ancestors, the Romans and the Etruscans, built amazingly beautiful towns and monuments, and the Renaissance artists took inspiration from these works of art to found a movement of beauty and culture which spread all over the world. But it's not just for beauty on a large scale that we are known all over the world. The idea of taste, harmony and perfection permeates our lives in many other ways. We look for beauty in small things, we recreate it in our homes and in our everyday lives if possible; we are possibly even obsessed with it, giving too much importance, sometimes, to appearances when it comes to building friendships and presenting ourselves to others. There are beautiful people of every age in Italy – beauty is not seen as something that solely belongs to youth. We have amazing parties and events, and we take perhaps an unusual amount of care over how places (and people) are decorated and presented for these occasions. In the realm of style we are renowned for designing and producing the very best jewellery, bags and shoes in the world.

Many of our buildings are incredibly beautiful, though, as is very often the case, there is a dark side, and the ugliness of some suburbs, new industrial towns and the painful presence of horrifying slums, immigration and nomad camps with no water or electricity, the scandal of rubbish in a beautiful town like Naples, tell stories of neglect and despair that we cannot ignore.

More and more, we are becoming a country of extremes, where the noble beauty of our ancient towns is preserved with high care but then some regions suffer from a shortage of funds and cannot provide the essential to the people who live there. But we could say the same for many other countries in the world, for a beautiful city like London or for the fairytale-like Paris, where poverty is constantly increasing, where the suburbs actually tell stories of misery and desperation typical of our modern times.

Thank God, for the moment beauty is still Italy's prerogative: with all its art and natural beauty, it has a lot to offer. It's good to see that new flight destinations are coming up every day with low-cost airlines: Rimini, Forlì, Pesaro, Brescia, Alghero are being discovered by the world's tourists. So at last it is possible to see things away from the most famous routes: there is more to Italy than what you see in the guide books.

Travellers are getting more demanding, they want to discover new places and smaller towns and regions that are not as known as the usual Sardinia, Tuscany or Veneto. Italy can offer a lot on a small scale: Rome and Venice and Florence are of course masterpieces, but then Ferrara, Urbino, Lecce, Caserta, Imperia, or our amazing Spa towns like Chianciano or Salsomaggiore are authentic treasures that are now being discovered, and there is so much beauty in these smaller, less known places.

After a long time of predominance of Tuscany over many other places in Italy, the world is discovering our hidden treasures: beautiful regions like Abruzzi and Marche, Apulia and Calabria, with their incredible seascapes, landscapes, history and food. But of course things are not that simple. People choose some regions renowned for art treasures over others, the services and hospitality in these places count, but most of all it's because of how the art is kept and exhibited.

With Italy being made up of regional governments as well as central powers, some regions are better than others in preserving and showing off their beauty. Tuscany of course has been one of those regions that have been able to preserve and even gradually improve its landscape and arts in the last century, hence all the interest from tourists. The concentration of art and beautiful scenery is also greater here than in other regions, but places like Calabria – part of Magna Grecia – which has wonderful coastline and impressive views, plus a lot of history, have only recently started to become favourite destinations for tourists.

Having a lot of tourists in some places and few in others has its drawbacks, naturally. First of all because a vicious circle seems to exist: some regions apply for grants and get them more easily than others because they 'sell' more and have a greater turnover of tourists. So, other regions, especially from the South, keep losing the opportunity to develop their tourism sector in a more organic way.

The other side effect is the complete flooding of tourists we get in some periods of the year in areas of North and Central Italy. As Dario Castagno wrote in his book *Too Much Tuscan Sun: Confessions of a Chianti Tour Guide*, the fact of having so much tourism in Tuscany can be quite a problem sometimes. Tourists come all year round and are not always entirely respectful of the beauty and the environment, of course, which means that our villages and towns can suffer from significant wear and tear by the masses of visitors concentrated mostly over six months of the year. But, again, things are slowly changing, important events are being organised all over the year so that people will find it interesting to travel at Christmas as well as Easter, and in February as well as May.

* * *

Keeping our treasures intact and preserved has of course been a priority in Italy for many years. That is why we have the *Soprintendenza dei Beni Culturali ed Artistici*.

This is an organisation that keeps a steady eye on the condition of our buildings, and tries, relatively successfully, to preserve art and architecture in Italy. This also concerns aspects of those buildings which are not listed or considered of special significance, but which contribute to the general aspect of a place. The *Soprintendenza* is very important and must be consulted before any changes can be made in homes or built properties. If you live in a Medieval or ancient town or village of some sort, and you have decided to open a restaurant, for example, then the first thing you will have to do is go to the office of the *Soprintendenza* and tell them what you have in mind. You will most certainly not be able to provide parking in a place that is visible from the street or change anything on the outside of the building.

Each region's *Soprintendenza* has a strict code of rules that people and institutions have to apply for any even tiny bit of work that they want to do on any property considered of historical value, but some people have been very critical of how we have managed to preserve the 'museum' that Italy is, by allegedly opposing progress.

To keep them quiet, we invented a really good Italian expression, in fact two: *'sviluppo sostenibile'* (low-impact progress) and *'turismo di qualità'* (quality tourism). These two are often connected.

We always talk about *sviluppo sostenibile*, especially in the press. This can mean anything from how to position a factory close to a large ancient town, to how to build an airport in the middle of a fantastic landscape. Yes, because *sviluppo sostenibile* can stop meaning a lot when there are big interests and big money involved in a project. This is also 'typical Italy'.

At the time of writing, a classic example of the clash between heritage preservation and 'progress' is underway: near Siena, to the South, politicians and local people have been discussing the extension of a small airport called Ampugnano. This aiport would have a few runways in the middle of an incredible landscape which also includes the famous San Galgano Abbey with no roof. A sixty-thousand-people town will never provide enough passengers for this project to make sense, and, if this goes ahead, the airport will probably be an elite place where politicians, actors and famous *Palio* jockeys fly in expensive planes to go from Milan to Siena to see the horse race. All this wouldn't bring work for people, it would bring pollution and noise, and a scar on the face of one of the most beautiful landscapes of the world. So, where is the *Soprintendenza* when big money is involved? How can we even consider extending Ampugnano after the lengths people have gone to to preserve Siena as it was in the Middle Ages paintings by Lorenzetti?

Let's hope the committee opposing this project (which the Sovicille people are very unhappy about) will win against the *casta senese*, the political elite. But the very fact that they are considering something like this is incredibly worrying.

There are many more questions that involve our artistic heritage. For example, the famous one: *lavori in corso*. I remember English visitors complaining about the fact that some buildings seem to be a work in progress forever. Here, again, it's a matter of grants from the State or from the regions. If they run out of money, it will take time for the region to send more money – it's simple bureaucracy. So let's say it's not strictly our fault. The politicians again need to be blamed for this.

It doesn't, of course, mean that we are not obsessed with beauty and ancient monuments. We are well aware that these are amongst our greatest assets and we do a lot to preserve and enhance these gifts our great artists gave us. So, if in some towns life can be difficult due to this obsessive will to keep everything as it used to be, we have to say that this obsession is very often the reason why the same towns are so rich and can count on tourism to live well and flourish.

But exactly what does it mean to live surrounded by tourists most days and not only for holidays? 'I don't mind at all' Duccio, who runs a ceramic shop in Siena told me, 'In fact, after the crisis which followed 9/11, it's comforting to see our streets flooded with visitors again. I won't lie to you saying that it's horrible to have the town "spoilt". Here most people have respect for our buildings and squares, and they also like buying things from my shop. Siena lives on tourism and its art: why should we complain?'

Roberta in Florence feels differently: she owns a restaurant, but still thinks tourism should be limited and organised more. 'Florence is always full of visitors, coaches everywhere and noise, dirt and bad behaviour are a daily thing in our town. I wish we could go back to the 'sixties, when tourism was just a nice addition to Florence and not a mass phenomenon'.

In the South of Italy, where tourism is a more recent aspect of life, things are different. The richness of these landscapes is very widely admired, but unfortunately sometimes the lack of funding makes it harder to offer enough decent 'hospitality' for tourists.

In Apulia, for example, although there are efforts being made to promote the beautiful sites and beaches, the region isn't ready for this yet. Maria Elena Tondi, who lives there, points out that there is a new interest about Apulia and the beaches are often full of people from Germany, America, France, Spain and the Orient, but Maria Elena adds 'even if interest in Apulia has grown, I don't find that there are enough places to host all the new people coming to us'.

However, Italy is making a good effort to improve its structures, but this doesn't always succeed. In fact, only the year 2006 saw a large increase, ten per cent, in the number of visitors coming from foreign countries, after about ten years without much change in the number of people visiting our peninsula. In fact, Spain and France have been doing much better than us if we count the number of foreign arrivals, and only 2006 and 2007 have actually seen an improvement in figures for Italy.

But if we look at *'turismo di qualità'*, the people who chose Italy are the art- and food-lovers, those who prefer the country *agriturismo* (farms where the guests can taste the produce and in some cases have a go at working on the land) to the big hotels; those who will visit the Medieval villages and churches and museums instead of clubbing or getting drunk on a beach.

Overall, the effort is paying dividends, and, if it's true that Italians go on holiday abroad more often than they did four years ago – even in spite of the Euro – it's also true that we can offer a lot of beauty and quality to those who choose Italy for their travels.

9. Sex: Do Italians Still Do It Better?

'I *know* Italian men who have understood everything about the secret of loving a woman, letting themselves go without being afraid ... Here is how loving friendships are born, passions, correspondences of senses ... a joyful, libertine way of loving, with a bit of sin which we have inherited from our Catholic morals.'

– Simonetta Losi, 42, from Siena

WHO DOESN'T REMEMBER MADONNA'S T-SHIRT? IT was the apotheosis of all clichés: the macho, the Latin male (and female), the sexiness of our language, music, food, good looks. All of that encapsulated in a T-shirt slogan that made history at the end of the 'eighties. The question of course is: are Italians still the most desired people in the world? Do they still do it better?

Well, I don't know about *better*, but Italian women certainly do it *more*: they are the most sexually active women in Europe, according to recent research. Fifty-nine per cent of them have sex at least once a week, followed by Czech women (fifty-seven per cent), Russian women (fifty-six per cent), French women (fifty-six per cent) and Spanish women (fifty-four per cent). Last in the list are Austrian women. The survey was conducted among twelve-thousand women by the European Association for Contraception, which also pointed out that only twenty-nine per cent of women in Italy use contraceptives, while the rest prefer the 'natural' method or the condom. So it's in fact quite surprising that we are low down on the list of countries for number of childbirths per year. But the figures show that we do enjoy sex once or more during a week, although this doesn't give away a lot about the quality of course!

We do have a reputation for being hot in bed and interested in sex. Actors with Italian names are often considered sexy: De Niro, Travolta, Pacino, Brando, Stallone are just a few that spring to mind, and our actresses are famously considered among the sexiest in the world, as Stephen Gundle notes in his excellent book describing the relationship between Italy, beauty and passion.

Italians certainly have a certain flair: we are supposed to be sexy and interested in lovemaking and … underwear. The latest corset launched by La Perla last Christmas is a red cage made of silky wires that wrap around the body for a very interesting effect (unfortunately the English don't think much of it, according to the *Times Magazine*, Sunday 16 December 2007).

But how is Italy in bed, really? Maybe I should rewrite the question: how is Italy 'in the car'? Yes, because for a long time now the car has been the main bedroom for a lot of couples. Mostly, but not entirely, young couples. When I said this to my husband-to-be he found it hard to believe. 'Why would people chose to make love in the back of a car when beds are much more comfortable?' asked Rob, raising an eyebrow. So I explained to him that often in Italy it's not a question of *choosing* to make love in a car. It's often the only option we've got!

Picture this: a twenty-five-year-old who lives at home with his parents finds a lovely girlfriend. They go out for a while. It's the end of summer. After going out to dinner, to the movies etc, they find themselves wanting to sleep together. Where do they go?

It's much too early to introduce the girlfriend or boyfriend to the family. No friends who have a free apartment at the moment. Not much money to book a room in a hotel (also, what would the hotel receptionist think?). Too dangerous to find an open air spot after the *Mostro di Firenze* stories (he killed many couples over a long period of time, they caught him, but who knows if another like him is out there?).

So, the car is the only option. It's mainly a front-seat affair: when you buy a car you need to know how the front seat reclines, it's one of the most important features for Italians when choosing a new car! Also, how much space do you have for your legs? Would it be comfortable enough for 'relaxing'?

If anybody felt like starting a survey on which country sells the most car fresheners, Italy would win by miles over everybody else. Our cars are temples of cleanness and emanate the most wonderful perfumes. But it doesn't have to be an Alfa Romeo or a Mercedes of course: a Fiat 500 can be right for quite a few acrobatic moments (and I am not talking only about the New Fiat 500).

This, let's call it, pastime, is as much part of our lifestyle as having parties for New Year's Eve or dressing up for Carnival: in fact, some local authorities have opened special covered, heated car parks where people can pay to go for some uninterrupted intimacy.

So, cars are our main choice if there's nowhere else to go. But after having introduced the partner to the family, things get easier. Sunday afternoons can easily become a moment of intimacy in the bedroom in the family home (the parents might go out for a stroll to give us privacy).

Does it all sound crazy to you? Well, get used to it: lots of things regarding our sex lives are quite unusual. We are a Catholic country, for a start, and you'll still find couples who don't use contraceptives *at all* and who build large families. Not very often but, it still happens.

I have to say that, although I know many people in Italy, north and south, I have only ever met two couples who thought that using contraception is wrong, They each have three children. The Pope's ideas on contraception are not very popular and I think none of my friends has ever cared about what the Pope thinks on this matter. Also, it's amazing how people in the south have changed now, and, while I come from a generation where among my many cousins, I am the only only child. I now have two children while some of my cousins in the South have only one, by choice, and my cousins in Florence also chose to have only one child. My aunt had twelve children, but her children have a maximum of three, and some have none).

You might also be surprised to hear that prostitution is considered quite a good career, in that for many men it's still the way to enjoy a certain freedom in sex. The right-wing Lega Nord mayor of the local authority, the *Comune di Villa Feraldi* near Imperia, has recently proposed to raise money for the council by renting the empty council houses to prostitutes, to take them off the streets and at the same time use the empty spaces. But the four-hundred people of the village didn't jump at the idea, especially the wives.

But sleeping with male or female prostitutes is not considered such a horrible thing: between fifty- and seventy-thousand people were working as prostitutes in Italy in the year 2000, of which about forty per cent were foreigners. And in the same year, an estimated nine million people admitted to having had sex with a prostitute, more than one in seven.

Sometimes I think that things haven't changed that much since when my grandmother said to me in the early 'eighties: 'Well, if your grandfather wants to experience some things I won't allow, then it's OK if he does that with a prostitute.' She was also telling me often that she didn't enjoy sex that much, and that her education, from strict parents, might have affected that. Of course, those were very different times, but is the Catholic view of sex still affecting us now?

It's hard to say as a general thing, but I know how much it has influenced my own choices, and those of the friends I grew up with. When we reached our teens, in the early 1980s, we had heard so much about not having sex until we were pretty sure about our feelings for our boyfriend, that we basically put it off for a long time. In fact, our way of behaving suggested that we were just the opposite, but it was all a cover-up. After a string of platonic relationships from fourteen to eighteen, I met somebody I thought fit the idea I had of a Real Boyfriend. Mature, quite a few years older than me, intelligent, kind, smart, funny *and* with a flat in the town.

I met him at a dinner party and he thought I was an experienced eighteen-year-old, which I wasn't at all. Thank God, a mutual friend explained to him that my experience with sex was limited to a few games on Sunday afternoons with my ex-boyfriend. And I fell in love with him in the most traditional way, which is why the idea of sex didn't scare me: it wasn't against my principles if I was really in love.

OK, it was the 'eighties. But half of the girls in my class in

Siena had started having sex at sixteen, so we girls from 'the country' were quite the exception.

I think that living in a small village made us different from our friends. But having Catholic families was another important factor. Although my mother and grandmother were very Catholic and my father and grandfather quite strict Communists, all of them had the same idea: they had taught us that in fact we should remain virgins until marriage. The idea of a white wedding with the right person, the idea of 'not letting anybody pick our flower until that day' was taught to us from a young age. Our mothers told us that a boyfriend would get tired of us if we slept with him. So we should keep him at bay and promise all good things to come after the wedding. Our fathers would just tell us having sex before marriage was wrong, and threatened us to throw us out of the house, as simple as that.

We didn't really hold these points of view ourselves, and we formed our own ideas about the love-sex connection and all that. Also, it became obvious in secondary school that lots of people had already done it anyway.

After finding the 'right person', for ages we would wonder if it wasn't against religion, and we would confess our sins on Sunday to the priest, hoping he would keep them to himself.

How is the attitude to sex in Italy twenty years later? How are modern Italian teenagers comparing to when my generation was sixteen? Interestingly, people seem to fall into two groups, which are reflected also by literature and the media.

On the one hand is the careless sex described in all its crudity as a way to react to a certain type of strict family education as well as social conventions of education. The other is poetic love, where sex is not the ultimate goal, and teenagers are looking more for affection than for a physical relationship.

103

There was a scandal in Italy when a 16-year old, Melissa Panarello, decided to write openly about her sex life in her diary. And she decided to publish it, without her surname, with a provocative title: *Cento colpi di spazzola prima di andare a dormire* (A hundred brush strokes before going to sleep). The book tells a lot about rebellion against a strict Sicilian education, about sex seen as a way of knowing and discovering the world of adults, but also as a series of sometimes meaningless experiences. On the other hand, Loredana Frescura opens up a different way of talking about teenagers and sex, with her own titles starting from *Elogio della Bruttezza* (Ode to Ugliness) to *Il mondo nei tuoi occhi* (The world in your eyes). Frescura talks about a fairytale-like way of expressing feelings, where sex is only a tender part of the evolution of a love story – something derived from our own teenage idea of sex somehow.

So, again, Italian teenagers, who bought lots of books by both authors, possibly have a bit of Melissa and a bit of Loredana in them. Because, whatever we say, the influence of Catholicism will always be part of us, even if we don't go to church and we criticise the way the Pope speaks on Sundays. (See Chapter on Religion.)

Now, if beauty, sex and sin are really entwined, then Italy *is* the land of love.

Some have written that the Mediterranean sunshine and a traditional morality together have given us an idea of love which is different from all other countries.

It is probably true, as some have written, that foreign men since quite long ago have formed an idea of the Italian woman as passionate, sensual, ready to accept her 'call' to become a mother, free from a constructed image that is often found abroad. And I think this is something British men still think: in fact, my husband is considered a lucky man among his workmates, especially for the fact he has an Italian wife. The model of the warm, natural, tactile woman who attracts and confuses, associated with Mediterranean countries, is somehow a constant one in men's imaginations.

When I sent my survey to men and women in Italy, a few of them talked about the 'Mediterranean sunshine' being in our eyes and giving us a special charm and tendency to be warm and intense. 'Italian men taste of earth, of worked soil, of long walks by night along the Palermo alleys, they have brown faces, tanned by the sun and not by a sunbed, they are distracted, silent, but at the same time they have a lot to say and they move their hands when they get fired up. They are serious and they are liars. A female friend of mine would say that they are full of contradictions: you think you have understood them but in fact they lied to you'. This excellent description given to me by a fellow journalist, Andrea Semplici, is in fact quite similar to the quote at the beginning, quoted by Simonetta Losi, another colleague.

She also added that Italian men are very generous and take a lot of pleasure in giving more than taking. 'Italian men know how to recognise beauty and have the wonderful gift of recognising beautiful things, of knowing how to share these with a woman, and they like making her feel good. The joy of being together, of spending time together, which I see every day in my *Contrada* [in Siena] is a very strong example. They give value to emotions, and to a sense of game, of irony, of the art of living which requires genius, elegance, reasoning and madness. All of this makes us live intensely, but also gives a sense of detachment which increases its fascination'.

I do agree with this point of view: I think that, with all our faults, we enjoy sex as we enjoy food and all the other pleasures of life. We read a lot about the crisis of emotions, of the couple, and even of the way men view their sexual power:

I think all this is part of Italy too, but our sense of togetherness has been saving us from becoming a nation in emotional crisis like many others in Europe. The increasing number of divorces and, on the other hand, the fall in numbers of weddings haven't applied to Italy as much as other countries: people still love getting married and also there are more and more long-term but unmarried couples forming, thanks to a new legislation which favours unmarried couples.

The view of Italian men and their relationships can be different from the outside: only a few months ago, the British press published a string of articles about the supposed 'crisis of the Italian male'. In particular, Richard Owen of *The Times* wrote in his article 'Mamma's Boys': 'Many Italian men feel sorry for themselves in twenty-first-century Italy – browbeaten, overworked and underpaid. Even the famous Latin lover is exposed as a myth.' Owen quotes a survey that seems to underline the sexual dissatisfaction of Italian women with their men's performances.

But this is not really what I found when discussing this question with fellow Italian women. Interviewing the Italians, it seems that our sex lives are quite healthily balanced between sentiment and transgression.

I think that the Italians are suspended between two peaks: that of tradition, of the Latin lover, of 'Italians do it better', and that of a new Italy where women have changed, are now more independent and know what they want. The model of the mother does not work as much as it used to, and those men who look for a mother-like partner can sometimes be bitterly disappointed. Nowadays marriage and family are not as important as they used to be; even if feminism hasn't had the same impact on women here as it has in other countries, a healthy freedom in our sex lives and a higher number of single women who want to work and give importance to their careers and independence have surely changed our way of behaving in relationships, especially in the North.

But some things will never change. The idea of the Italian woman as warm, sexy, curvy, protective and loving, skilled in the bedroom and in the kitchen, is hard to replace. And still many men believe in it and look for it in a potential partner. In my own circle of friends, a few men who found a stable partner declared that they had managed to find 'what you can't find in a woman anymore now' – beauty, intelligence, and skills like cooking, cleaning and taking care of children.

'...*una donna così è rara,*' (a woman like this is rare), said Nicola to me about his girlfriend.

So, on one side, most men seem to be still looking for a woman who responds to a traditional image they have built up over the years, on the other side women are changing and are often not ready to 'replace the mother' for their men. And for some, this is the key to our Italian men's dissatisfaction, in a way. This is where the foreign woman comes in: there are more and more couples formed by an Italian man and a partner from East Europe or the Orient, from Africa or South America. This is apparently because the increased independence of Italian girls doesn't appeal to our men as much as the 'geisha' idea of a woman, where the partner or wife certainly might go out to work but, when back home, she reverts to that model of traditional, warm, somehow submissive partner who cooks and stands by her man in sexy clothes.

Is this why Italian men are in a crisis, why they seem to have lost their identity?

Well, not really, judging by the ninety or so comments that readers posted about Richard Owen's 'Mamma's Boys' article, which quoted Fabio Capello as an atypical Italian

New Man. Both Italian men and women commented that modern Italian men are still in good shape, thank you very much, often sexy, warm and romantic, and yes, they like taking care of their mothers too, 'She took care of me and I don't want to put her in a home'. Italian men used words like 'envy', women in Italy said that their men are actually pretty good and at least they don't drink themselves silly. Interestingly, quite a few British women commented: 'I would have an average Italian man any day…'.

Of course, like everywhere else, in Italy people sleep with prostitutes, commit adultery and surf the net for sex; they chat online often with the sole aim of meeting and having sex with a complete stranger (something that seems to be quite fashionable in Italy in recent years).

All of this is part of our nation too, and divorce and adultery are on the rise. But, like with many other sides of Italian life, emotions are often contradictory in our country, and so, if on one side we could say that there have been more divorces in these last years, it's also true that romance, flirting, courting are back in fashion. Also, as I found out in my research for my book about fidelity, this is considered more and more a value among couples of all ages.

After the 'seventies, when everything from cinema to literature was reflecting a lack of values and a sense of 'nothing' which seemed very worrying, the 'nineties seemed to be a return to the pleasure of monogamy. So, if our media seems to demonstrate a constant interest in naked young women, our family values seem to get stronger.

Interestingly, also, while *The Times* published 'that article', and another one where an English woman describes a fling with a young, dashing Italian man only to discover that he was vain and 'mamma dependent', the *Telegraph* published an article entitled 'An amorous offer you can't refuse'.

Its author, Casilda Grigg wrote a brilliant analysis of 'how to do it the Italian way', or how to learn flirting again. Flirting has become rare in the UK, she argues, due to a culture where sex is sometimes still considered a forbidden side of our personality. According to her article, the fear of making a fool of one's self is still quite strong in the British, while, according to research, smiling and making eye contact can be enough. Casilda, in order to learn more about flirting, went to meet Marco Gambino, a forty-five-year-old Sicilian actor who apparently 'has a gift for making a woman feel desirable'.

She writes about the way Marco looks at her, making her feel important, listening to her and also holding her gaze with no fear – people tend to avoid eye contact because they are scared of it. She also notices that he hasn't been drinking one drop of alcohol.

The article goes on to describe the signals that Marco uses to impress and fascinate her, and then concludes with a list of Gambino's Flirting Tips: they include using your eyes, moving with confidence, using body language, being more tactile, lighthearted and playful, taking care of your appearance, not making too many jokes or talking too much, and, very importantly, listening to the other person.

Knowing Italian men, I have to say that this art of flirting is still alive and well in my country, while indeed it may have been lost in the UK. Italian men and women know how to use their charms and love flirting. They make you feel important, essential in their lives. They are not afraid of looking deep into your eyes.

So, for what it's worth, in my experience, Italy still is The Land of Love, and, although my husband asks me why I chose an English man after trying the Italians, I remind him that our love and passion was born in the heart of Tuscany, and that we often return there. In fact, as my friend Andrea Semplici put it, my husband is now more Sicilian than English. That's the power of true Italian passion that can indeed change the world … and the British! Although I have to say that I intensely love the Britishness of a light smile, of having the door opened for me and of getting a lovely bunch of flowers just to say 'I love you'.

This spectacular procession in Clerkenwell for the Madonna del Carmine festival takes place on the third Sunday of July, and is the most popular Italian religious event in the UK. Many Italian associations come to take part. (Photo by Annalisa Coppolaro-Nowell)

The rows of people in costumes for the Palio horserace in Siena are suggestive and fascinating. (Photo by Joe Nowell)

Viareggio Carnival 2006: Berlusconi as a bunny girl carrying the sign of Festa de l'Unità, the festival organised every year by the Left in every Italian town.
(Photo by Annalisa Coppolaro-Nowell)

A lute player at the Medieval Feast in Murlo, every first weekend of June. The event comes to life in this village, the symbol of Medieval architecture in the South of Siena. (Photo by Annalisa Coppolaro-Nowell)

Lupompesi, my village, near Murlo. The photo was taken by my nephew from the hill where part of the family olive grove stands: a beautiful viewpoint. (Photo by Alex Young)

A demonstration against the expansion of Siena Airport, taking place outside the National Gallery, London in 2008. Protestors argue that it would mean the end of an unspoilt region. (Photo by Annalisa Coppolaro-Nowell)

Images from the South: Joe and his cousin Modestino playing in the streets of Friuni, near Tocco Caudio, my father's birthplace near Benevento. Earthquakes and poverty have forced many people from this area to move North. (Photo by Annalisa Coppolaro-Nowell)

One of the fantastic dinner parties at my aunt Giulia's house near Florence. From the right: cousin Maria Luisa, my father Cosimo, cousins Maurizio and Cinzia, aunt Giulia, cousin Silvia, Franco and me. (Photo by Annalisa Coppolaro-Nowell)

Elderly Sicilians sit and chat on an autumn afternoon. Friendship, warmth and family make the silver years very enjoyable. (Photo by Gabriele Fanetti/FotoModerna Siena)

Francesco picking grapes in our vineyard on a warm October afternoon. One more occasion to have fun with our friends, enjoy the sunshine and celebrate the fruits of our land. (Photo by Annalisa Coppolaro-Nowell)

A shop in Via di Città, Siena, selling fruit and regional specialities in the heart of this beautiful historical town. (Photo by Annalisa Coppolaro-Nowell)

The fantastic painted stucco ceiling in the Palazzo Vecchio, Florence. (Photo © Mike Longhurst/Rex Features)

Early morning at a Sicilian fish market: the freshest, juiciest tuna, swordfish and shellfish are sold here from 5 in the morning in a joyful atmosphere. (Photo by Gabriele Fanetti/FotoModerna Siena)

Fabio Capello, England football coach. A charming family man and art collector, he is one of the symbols of successful Italy abroad. (Photo © Rex Features)

Waiting for the World Cup Final, July 2006. From top right: Katerina and Tommaso. Second row from right: Bernardo, Joe, Mattia, Antonio and Gregory. Front from right: Francesco and Filippo, sitting on the stairs of our Tuscan home. (Photo by Annalisa Coppolaro-Nowell)

Lake of Como: an early morning image on the road from Milan to Livigno, a beautiful ski resort in the North of Italy. (Photo by Paolo Minoli)

From right: Andrea Bocelli, Laura Pausini and Eros Ramazzotti. Three different styles of singing love, for three hugely popular singers, who represent Italian creativity to the rest of Europe and the world. (Photo © Camilla Morandi/Rex Features)

The Doge's Palace Courtyard, Venice (detail). This magnificent Gothic building was probably designed by Filippo Calendario. The elegant façade, arches and statues are an enduring testament to the skill of Italian architects. (Photo by Paolo Minoli)

The Old and the New: hard to say if the New Fiat 500, European Car of the Year 2008, will over-take the cute old model in popularity. Personally, I drive my 1972 red one, just like this one, and lovingly keep my father's 1968 with great pride!
(Photo © Matt Vosper/Auto Express/Rex Features)

Galleria Ferrari, Maranello (Modena). The style and design of an icon are cel-ebrated in this wonderful gallery, open since 1990. Over 40 models are dis-played, each exuding a distinctive class and charm. (Photo by Annalisa Coppolaro-Nowell)

La Dolce Vita in Olympia, London. There's always a space dedicated to Alfa Romeo, Fiat, Ferrari or Maserati in this amazing London show about Italian food and lifestyle, taking place every March. (Photo by Annalisa Coppolaro-Nowell)

Italy's controversial Prime Minister Silvio Berlusconi campaigning during the April 2008 elections. (Photo © Marianella Marco/Rex Features)

In Lupompesi: a warm handshake between Murlo's mayor Antonio Loia and our priest Giacinto di Polito. Guareschi's era of feuds between Don Camillo and Peppone must be really over then! (Photo by Annalisa Coppolaro-Nowell)

10. Sports - 'Forza Italia': Corruption, Excellence and Fabio Capello

'It's now up to Italy to bring England back to success'

> – BBC News, December 2007, just before Fabio Capello was appointed coach of the England football team

THE YEAR 2006 WAS POSSIBLY ONE OF THE WORST for Italian football. Juventus, the Old Lady, was relegated in the *Serie* B after a huge match-fixing scandal was discovered. Their *Scudetto*, the prize given to the winning *Serie* A team, was taken away from them. Other teams like Milan and Fiorentina were fined and many points were taken off in the 2006–2007 season.

One month later Italy won the World Cup for the fourth time, the only National team to achieve this in Europe. That same season, Ferrari and Michael Schumacher were crowned World Champion in Formula 1 for the seventh time. They both became the highest-winning champions in Formula 1 history.

I think these few lines sum up the history of Italian sports quite well. Italy is the country with the best players in the world and the worst sport scandals ever recorded; where a match will suddenly stop because a police officer has been killed in the stadium; while Valentino Rossi wins the World title again, becoming the star of motorbike racing with his 88 GP wins and seven world titles.

This mixture of excellence and scandal is possibly what makes our sport world unique, but the results speak for themselves. No other team has won as much as Ferrari, and of course, as many would agree, Ducati is the best motorbike of all times.

We excel at the Olympics: our country often appears among those with the most medals won: we win in athletics, rowing, fencing, etc. For a nation with (presumed) low self-esteem all these results are great, and sport is an important way to affirm that we can be better than other nations. Of course we have our low points: in tennis we haven't managed to have a champion since the years of Panatta and Bertolucci, for example.

In recent months, Fabio Capello being appointed coach of the England national team provided a huge talking point to the media, with interesting results. Stereotypes emerged, often in a funny way. *The Times* pictured him as a Mafia boss and their headline read: 'You don't mess with Fabio'. And the coaching team, comprised of Italians, also provoked some resentment in the English observers. But in the UK they had to accept that this team has a lot to learn from Italy and from a man who has been working with Juventus and Real Madrid.

Never mind the scandals; Italian football – as *Football Italiano* on Channel 5, with its sexy, Italian presenter, amply proves – can be the best in the world. Capello of course is not only a football coach: he also represents a certain idea of Italy. He has been married for forty years and has a happy family life (in fact *The Times* said that having a united family is the strongest source of pride for him), but, most surprisingly he's an art collector. He owns important works by Kandinsky and Chagall, and, quite amazingly, has managed to get his footballers interested in art. Jonathan Zebina, the Juventus defender, now has his own art gallery after Fabio started to talk about art in the changing room!

He was still a player when he began to collect works by the futurist Giorgio de Chirico. He has compared Spanish football to Cy Twombly's art and is a good friend of Piero Pizzi Cannella, a great Italian contemporary artist. Would you see any of the England footballers being interested in futurist art? Well, you never know: with Capello as a coach miracles could happen. Although the writer Hunter Davies, who wrote about Gascoigne and Rooney, has commented that from 1972 to the present day he has never seen art of any note on the walls of the many footballers houses he visits, Fabio Capello might be just the man to change this sad, sad reality.

Certainly, a man like Capello, often described as a 'natural-born winner', is a good example of how Italy can be fascinatingly diverse and deeply interesting. Although some clichés happily still apply: Capello's mum, for starters, has told the media that she's not happy about her son going off to the UK at all. Never mind the £6 million he earns every year: she will still live in her two-bedroom flat and wait for her son to phone her every day, like he's been always doing.

But sports in Italy are much more than what you read about in the papers. They say that we are a lazy nation, when it comes to sweating in the gym, but there is a reason for that. Just like eating, sport for us is mainly a social occasion, and a team thing. So you won't often see people eating by themselves in a *trattoria*, just like you won't see many lonely runners in a park. But then, if you go to any village you will find a keen group of hikers, for example. There will also be a football field, and in this field there will be a tiny team of eight-year-olds practicing for their next match.

When my family and I got back from Italy after our year spent there, the children were disappointed to find that in London only the big football clubs have what we call a *vivaio*, a training programme for young champions. Of course getting into these clubs is very hard. In Tuscany my sons had been playing for two teams and loving it. These were local teams; they didn't win very often, but they took their training very seriously, had proper kits and bags with logos, showers and well-organised outings. They appeared in the papers, which give space to all categories, from A to *Promozione*, to all these small tournaments between villages.

Is this another advantage of 'campanilism'? Possibly. The local team involves not just sporty people, but retired men and women, local housewives, shopkeepers and priests: in one way or another, if you feel like taking part, there is something for you to do: maybe taking photos, writing the posters, calling the parents to advertise an event, organising and cooking for a party, sending formations and scores to the press, etc.

Sport in Italy is mainly a social thing: like in many other fields, we think that practising sports by one's self is slightly sad, as opposed to the 'team' idea, where each person can give a bit of themselves for the team.

And, if violence can occasionally blight the big stadiums in Italy, this never happens at smaller-scale events. The atmosphere of a local football match is that of a party, some rivalry is of course there, but it has a friendly face. Often the children don't even hope to get to a larger team, they just enjoy training and playing and seeing their names in the paper once a month.

The scandals such as Moggi and Juventus of course make headlines and make people talk in bars, but when the weekend comes, people meet in the local football field to watch their grandson or granddaughter play. Going to see our *Serie* A team play is a treat, we can do that maybe once a year, but the fun part is meeting with your village friends to see a mountain-bike race or a local horse race, or taking part in a 'parents against sons' football match in the church football field.

Encouraging our children to play sport doesn't mean making them hope they will become Totti or Del Piero or Cannavaro: it's part of healthy lifestyle idea, of course, but mainly it's the social side that counts. That's how our children don't kill each other in gang fights but prefer a healthy row after a match, and all will end well at the local bar, eating pizza or sipping a Chinotto.

Italian schools encourage sports too. Big, beautiful gyms and sports fields are in nearly every school and they are also used by local people for evening keep-fit classes or by the local volleyball team for their training sessions.

In 1968 *Giochi della Gioventù* were invented: all the local authorities, or *Comuni*, of Italy take part in this. The idea is that the school children who excel in the qualifiers held in the schools will compete with similar age groups coming from other towns in the region for a cup or medal given to the athletes and to their schools. This was launched for two reasons: to promote sports for young people and to give a reason for the state to help build more sport facilities for schools. Both aims were achieved.

It's a great satisfaction for a student to be part of these

Giochi della Gioventù: I remember qualifying among the first three in the *corsa campestre* (an endurance race held in the fields) and in the 200-metres race when I was twelve, but then I was eliminated in the big race in Siena. But having the honour to represent my school at the *Giochi della Gioventù* was great source of pride for me.

Now these games are called *Giochi Sportivi Studenteschi* and include all the sports actually practised in schools: athletics, gymnastics, swimming, skiing, football, basketball, netball and volleyball. Now they also include Italians who are resident abroad.

Our idea of group sports comes from ancient times. The South of Italy, modern Calabria, Apulia and Sicily, being under Greek domination, saw many Olympic games in classical times. The winning athletes sipped local wine and tasted local foods, and this is when the fun of competing became so important to the people in these areas. Artworks from Roman and Etruscan times depict horse races and athletes, and from these ancient examples right through the Fascist era to the present day, Italy has always seen sport and competition as something positive for the body as well as for the soul.

Since the birth of Italy in 1861, our governments promoted physical education. The Minister De Sanctis in fact, during that same year, founded the first teacher training course for PE teachers, and in 1867 a course for women wanting to become physical education teachers. After being introduced as a school subject in some regions well before 1861, PE was approved as an obligatory activity in every school in 1950.

Famously, the fascists were possibly the most keen on funding sports activities, believing in the idea that a strong boy will make a strong soldier. But women were also encouraged: the sporty woman started to be found pleasing in the 'twenties, and she would also be useful to the state if she was well.

Very soon, the Church opposed this, believing that it would take women's interest away from having children and taking care of the family. Undoubtedly, though, under Mussolini, much effort was put into the setting up of associations like the ENEF, *Ente Nazionale Educazione Fisica*, founded in 1923. As a nation, because of this approach to sports in schools, but also thanks to the thousands of sports clubs and football associations for young people, it seems quite natural that we get excellent results. From chess to darts, boules to motor racing, excellence in sport is an everyday thing in our country.

So why is it that our sport scandals are also the most talked about in the world? I believe it comes with the baggage: if we were a second-class country with second-class football or racing, possibly there wouldn't be so much interest towards the the dark side of Italian sport.

For a while Giuliano Moggi became a regular feature on front pages all over the world. His involvement with Juventus and with match-fixing, the subsequent arrest, his confessions and stories managed to put the *Vecchia Signora* (The Old Lady), the most popular, prize-winning, prestigious and oldest football club in Italy, in a bad light.

If you count the number of football fans in Italy, over half of them support Juventus. All through my primary and secondary school years I was in a class composed entirely of Juventus fans bar one, Monica, a Fiorentina fan who had great courage in standing up for herself and declaring that 'since we are in Tuscany why should we be fans of a Turin football club?' But Juventus were winning everything, and still are. There was nothing better for the fans of all the other *Serie* A clubs than to realise that Juventus too had their faults; that the reason why they were winning all the time was that they were CHEATING!

But Juventus proved their true colours by winning everything in *Serie* B, going back to A and being one of the three clubs fighting for the *Scudetto* in 2008.

Milan, Fiorentina and other clubs were involved in this scandal, and they also had to pay with points and shame for this.

In a way, the press loved all this, because it was a way to bring down our sport: it was like saying: 'OK, Italians might be good at sport, but look what's really going on!'

Of course, here is the good part of the scandal: it happened in Spring-Summer 2006, the year of the World Cup. Then there was the Big Question: would a National team comprised of shameful players involved in terrible scandals even win a match in the coming World Cup?

They did, and won and won again, and got to the final. Somehow nobody was surprised. Because nobody really ever questioned the value of our players. A goalkeeper (from Juventus) often described in the international press as the best in the world, Buffon, is a good start. Names like Camoranesi, Del Piero, Pirlo, Toni, Totti and Cannavaro just spoke for themselves. Class and style, concentration and reliability, imagination and supreme skills were their weapons against the attacks of the media, against all the things, true and false, written about them.

Italy won: pictures of parties held all over the world the night of 9 July hang now in all Italian clubs all over the world, in every home, in the heart of all of us. That win had many meanings. Especially one: it was the perfect way to show the real value of our sportsmen.

But football is not our only passion in sport – although it's by far Italy's favourite.

Ferrari and Ducati are of course the other icons of our sporting success. Both as red as our passion for the good things in life and for good quality design, Ferrari and Ducati have been igniting the racetracks for several decades. They have won more than any other team in the world. Ferrari has beaten every record. From Prost to Senna, from Schumacher to Raikonnen, the best racing drivers have chosen Ferrari to excel.

Ferrari does not ignore defeat: its mechanical problems made Kimi very cross more than once in the 2007 season, but he still managed to win. Ferrari, in spite of the bad times, *is* Formula 1's most loved team in the world. And everywhere in the world owning a Ferrari is considered a sign of success, of having achieved great things in life.

In Italy we measure the state of our economy by the number of Ferraris that are parked in our towns. If you see plenty of them, then things are going well.

Its design, speed, class, accessories and price tag make this car an object of desire. Jeremy Clarkson is on cloud nine and purrs like a grinning cat when driving one along a smooth North Italian road.

Ducati is another symbol of excellence in our sports: motor racing is represented by this red motorbike, described by my sister-in-law Michèle as "The best motorbike in the world ....with its wonderful, wonderful noise...."(she's an expert).

Then there is Valentino Rossi of course. His recent win at the Mugello circuit in Florence has proved how much love Italy has for him: 96,000 adoring fans went to follow the race. His tight leather trousers with The Doctor emblazoned across the back and his childlike smile are loved in Italy and everywhere else. The popularity of motorbike racing in Italy is largely due to him, on one side, and to Ducati's victories on the other.

Valentino is the son every mother would like: well, at least if he changed jobs. He's funny, successful, cute, clever and fame hasn't gone to his head. And the fact that he takes the name of Italy abroad, representing yet another successful icon of our sport, is very important to us. Along with Rossi, two other motorbike champions are Italian: Marco Melandri and Loris Capirossi – two more contemporary icons of motor sport who represent Italy all over the world.

Our success in motor sports is not just a modern-day phenomenon: Giacomo Agostini on his MV Agusta first and Yamaha later is considered perhaps the greatest Grand Prix rider of all time. He had a career of 17 years and won an incredible 15 world Grand Prix titles in the Sixties and the Seventies. He was also the first motorcyclist recognized by the World Sports Academy. He's one of the greatest personalities ever to have competed in motorbike racing – and, thanks to his extremely good looks and a champion's aura, loved all over the world.

* * *

So, if you do want to live like an Italian, fall in love with a Ferrari, play some football on Sunday, watch the *Azzurri* play, and remember: you are in a country where sport is considered essential, but where going to see a match on Sunday doesn't necessarily mean *Serie* A. The essential part of sport for Italians is sharing, being together and celebrating together.

Our stadiums have become safe places again. And our country is enjoying sport more than ever before. It's true that from time to time violence raises its ugly head in the big stadiums, and some people go to matches to confront the fans of the opposing team, but remember that this is the exception, not the rule. The Italian Parliament has approved a specific law, no.41, on 4 April 2007, outlawing violence: the fans who cause trouble will be banned from watching football, will have to pay fines, and generally be excluded from the pleasure of attending sports with their friends. The same law includes extra financial help for all schools in Italy who want to introduce new sporting activities, and supports all sports among young people.

11. Music: The Language of Music is Italian - A Short History of Excellence

> 'Music's debt to Italy is as great as that of Painting'
>
> – The Oxford Companion to Music

SHALL WE LOOK AT ANOTHER STEREOTYPE? OK: 'Italy, The Land of Music'. The greatest tenor of our age, Pavarotti, died in 2007 and the media are already asking who will be the next Luciano. But Italy has another ace up its sleeve. He's called Andrea Bocelli, He's considered the world's biggest-selling classical artist, with over fifty-five-million albums sold. This remarkable, sexy singer from Tuscany who became blind when he was very young sings like an angel. Italy has produced yet another musical phenomenon after centuries of operatic tradition. But something must have gone wrong somewhere: most of our youths don't know much, if anything, about classical music, they don't appreciate opera and don't really have a musical culture outside of the mainstream. In fact, state TV has recently produced an ad sponsored by the Government to promote the knowledge of classical music, which stars Uto Ughi, our most famous violinist.

My neighbour and friend Francis Florent remembers that in the post-war period some Italians he knew would gather in each other's homes and would stand up at the end of the meal to sing opera 'at the drop of a hat', as he puts it. That's certainly not something you'll see now. Most young people don't really recognise famous arias and barely know the names of our composers. There has been such a fuss in Italy around pop music in recent years, it has put classical music distinctly in the shade, so even those young people who may have begun to develop an interest have sometimes been put off it by their friends who think that classical music is old-fashioned and not a 'cool' thing to listen to.

But luckily with the new generation things are changing again. Young people are learning instruments again, and, after a long time when music was not considered as an important discipline by our secondary schools, recently it has been reintroduced more significantly into the curriculum.

While for sport there have been grants to schools from the state over the years, music was often considered not as important: now, though, secondary schools have introduced afternoon piano lessons for groups of motivated children, outings to concerts and music centres, and from the age of eleven children are taught the recorder as a regular practice all over Italy. We used to do it at my secondary school, in fact, years ago. We also used to listen to classical music at school and our teachers made a point of teaching us to recognise and appreciate different periods and composers.

Since the year 2000, together with other relatively new classical singers, Andrea Bocelli himself has become somehow the promoter of change: he's known among young people for a mixture of pop and classical music, and he's reviving interest in Puccini and Verdi among other world-famous Italian composers. The music of Palestrina, Monteverdi, Vivaldi, Scarlatti, Puccini, Rossini, Albinoni, Corelli, performers like Paganini, music directors like Riccardo Muti, singers like Tebaldi or Luciano Pavarotti himself and opera composers like Verdi, Bellini, Rossini, Donizetti, Puccini and Mascagni show that our music has been at the forefront of the classical genre throughout much of its history.

Far from the likes of Caruso or Gigli, Italy today is offering some new names like Ludovico Einaudi and Cecilia Gasdia. But we still have some work to do if we want to continue being the land of music and offering fresh new talent.

Italy, of course, has an incredibly prestigious musical tradition. It's no surprise that, all over the world, the key language for music students to learn is Italian. Even basic words like *opera*, *concerto*, *orchestra*, *aria*, *soprano*, come from our language, and notational terms such as *allegro*, *assai*, *andante*, *mosso*, *agitato*, *largo*, *vivace* in most pieces of music are Italian.

Many important classical music festivals are organised in Italy annually, and attract millions of people from everywhere in the world. So how did Italy become the Land of Music? Is it really this magical mix of sun, sea and sentiment that inspired Italians to make such wonderful music through the centuries? Surely these elements have had some importance. In Italy there is a famous saying that goes: '*Canta che ti passa*' (sing and it will all be alright): in fact, our greatest eighteenth-century songs were written in the South, and even in the twentieth century this passion for music in the South inspired pieces such as 'O *sole mio*', '*Santa Lucia*', '*Funiculi Funicula*' and 'Come Back to Sorrento'. With all its problems, the South of Italy has always had a talent for singing. But there are of course other elements: above all the genius of Italian instrument-makers and our creativity generally in the field of music have played a vital part, too.

In fact, many bricks have built the magnificent cathedral of our classical music. Incredible composers, creativity, poetry and a general love of beauty that is so strongly connected with the Italian people are, I think, the most important ones.

But let's start from the basics: the instruments. Musical-instrument production has always been part of Italy's musical heritage. The piano was invented by the Italian Cristofori in Florence in 1709: he called it *Gravicembalo col piano e forte* (a harpsichord with soft and loud). The method of hammers substituting the plucking of quills of the harpsichord was ingenious and, although a century before Cristofori there was a Dutch instrument with the same sort of system, our Cristofori is universally recognised as the creator of the pianoforte.

Today there is still a very active musical-instrument production industry in Italy, in towns like Bologna, Cremona, Florence, Ancona and Macerata. The best guitars, organs, accordions and pianos are made in Italy. A new market for synthesisers, sequencers and modulos, acoustic and electric guitars and wind and string instruments occupy an important place in our economy. It is also a growing market, which, in 2005 was up 2.1 per cent on the previous year, giving thousands of jobs and an export share of 50 per cent.

* * *

Many music genres began in Italy. Apart from Christian music that originated in the fourth century, opera, which dates back at least seven centuries, is certainly the most universally recognised Italian music and, interestingly, it was always popular among all of the social classes in Italy, while in other places it was exclusively a thing for the rich nobility.

Our country was divided of course, but united by language, religion since the thirteenth century, and by a rich vernacular literature. People began to create music in the form of poetry and songs in the Middle Ages. In the thirteenth and fourteenth centuries Italy had its own *Trovatori* arising from influence of the French Troubadours, and *Menestrelli*; more popular singers who also sang at court and in the streets. Part-singing was born in the form of *Frottola*, a popular unaccompanied song and there was *Canto carnascialesco* (carnival song) and *Laude Spirituale* or popular devotional song. All these forms were the result of a marriage between poetry and music, in a period where Dante and Petrarch were producing incredible literary works. The *Amor cortese*, Courteous Love, was the basis of a way of looking at beauty and sentiment with quite a modern spirit.

So, can we actually say that enjoying life and love is at the heart of our wonderful music tradition? According to music historians, it's very likely. The very joyful *Ballata*, for example, was a medieval choral form to be sung and danced at the same time, while the *Caccia* (or 'hunt') was a lively two-voice hunting song sung in canon. These, together with the *Madrigal*, had a noticeable rhythm and the lyrics were often poems. These compositions were particularly advanced for the time. 'The music was remarkable for its rhythmic variety, necessitating a series of note-divisions much more elaborate than that of other countries at the same period, and a consequent special manner of notation … A great variety of instruments was, at different times, called on to take part in the performance of these compositions', underlines the *Oxford Companion to Music* in its ample chapter on Italian music history. It seems that Italy was more advanced in many ways than other countries, and this of course led to the large influence that our music has always had.

The birth of *a cappella* singing in the sixteenth century, thanks to Palestrina, and that of opera still in Italy in the following century, showed again how much the Italian influence managed to change the history of world music. Also, these two forms put choral singing into a secondary position and favoured the solo voice. From here to creating beautiful operas there was only a step.

Of course other countries, like Germany, have contributed beautiful music to the opera genre as well as other incredible classical pieces, but I think the fact that ours was the original language of opera, even when written in other countries, is quite symbolic.

It is not entirely clear when Italian music terminology started to be used all over the world for music notation, for voices, tempos, musical instruments and other fields of classical music; according to various sources such as *The Oxford Companion to Music*, the reason for this is simply that many composers who started to write sheet music were Italian and this contributed to the spreading of our music terminology across the world. Today, with the exception of a small number of French and German terms, Italian remains the lingua franca of music everywhere, as it has been for several centuries.

Other fields of music, possibly lesser known, have also seen the strong influence of Italy: by the eleventh century music scholars had devised a system of sight-singing, while it was an Italian, Petrucci, who invented a practical music printing process at the end of the fifteenth century. The violin family of instruments was also devised in Italy (its greatest creators are still in Cremona), as was solo singing, otherwise known as *bel canto*. Music schools were introduced in Italy first, and they evolved into what we now call *conservatorio*.

'It will be seen that Music's debt to Italy is as great as that of painting', concludes the Oxford Companion to Music, which of course places the invention of opera in Italy and notes how significant the Renaissance in Florence was in bringing about the birth of new forms of music of invaluable importance.

So, it seems that Italy has always had a high place in the world's culture. The merit, for music, also has to go to the special sound of our language, which seems especially sweet if accompanied by beautiful music. I often find that the adult students who choose to come to my Italian classes in London do so because they love travelling to Italy, they tell me that Italian is such a musical language and they just love its sound intensely. They might or might not know opera, but they all agree on this particular aspect. Even the sound of my name often seems to have an effect on foreigners: firstly, there was my husband who commented on my beautiful name (but it might have been a way to chat me up, of course!). But often in London I find that people speaking different languages (Chinese, Albanian, Farsi, to name but a few) say that 'Annalisa' sounds especially nice.

Our love of life and beauty, together with the sound of our language and the natural imagination of our people has always been part of the foundation of the Italian musical tradition. Of course, a series of historical elements have played an essential part: the importance of the Middle Ages in Italy, then the development of the Renaissance in Central Italy, and then a very strong Romantic movement have all contributed to the evolution of our musical canon.

As for other fields, unfortunately we tend to live on the past glory of our classical music, as for many years our pop music, which is not great, has been regarded by the young people in Italy as *the* thing to listen to; our young music students mostly want to create their own pop bands or become solo artists. The prospect of becoming the New Eros Ramazzotti or Laura Pausini (our best-selling artists in Italy and abroad) is still what makes kids study singing or music. It's a common thing in every country: fame is the main objective, and since you don't see many classical artists making the news or appearing in glamour magazines, pop seems the way to go.

In Italy, pop of course holds a huge attraction. The arrival of X *Factor* in Italy has emphasised this fact. But there are other ways to make a name for yourself in the pop music world in Italy. For example, taking part in the Sanremo Music Festival.

Possibly the most popular in Italy, the festival was founded almost sixty years ago, and for a time had a somewhat trashy reputation, which it's only now beginning to put right. Big names – both Italian and foreign pop acts – are going to Sanremo again, drawn by the festival's renewed prestige. It goes on for almost a week and is a spectacle of colours, flowers, evening dresses, beauty and music. Everybody watches it, either to criticise it or to enjoy the performances: but, a bit like Miss Italia, few people miss it. A presenter's career is 'complete' if he or she is invited to host the Sanremo Festival, and big names like Zucchero or Vasco Rossi have emerged from this competition. Lots of young musicians dream of singing on the stage of Sanremo, few dream of performing at La Scala.

Happily, new music schools and academies have opened up in recent years, although, unfortunately, in some periods the history of music hasn't held much importance in our schools generally. Music education in Italy has predominantly been quite elitist: we may have the best music academies and conservatories in the world, but until recently our primary and secondary schools didn't actually devote that many hours to the teaching of music. Recently, the study of a musical instrument like the recorder has been reintroduced from the age of eleven, and more secondary schools are offering music seminaries and extra-curricular music activities, but back in the 'seventies and 'eighties there was a distinct lack of interest from our young people, due to the fact that our schools were not prioritising music enough. A big contrast with the nineteenth and early twentieth centuries, when opera was enjoyed by nearly everybody in Italy: my own great-grand father Alessandro, a land-owner and local councillor, was intensely passionate about it. He used to have a big radio which we still keep in our salon now, so he could listen to the performances broadcast by the state radio every other day. He had all the librettos and, although he could not afford to go to the concerts often, he encouraged his children to learn instruments. My mother is called Amneris Tosca and she and her cousin Norma were both deliberately given operatic names.

Somehow after the Second World War there was a general decline in people's interest this form of art, and classical music went back to being something mainly for the rich.

On a recent trip to Siena, I was talking to a friend of mine, Graziano Bernini, who is a well-known painter. He's very proud of his peasant origins and noted the fact that even now in small Tuscan villages it's very unusual to find a piano in a house, while a house in Siena or Florence is quite likely to have one.

My children each play an instrument and have already passed some music exams, but having been a teenager in the 'eighties (possibly Italy's worst-ever decade for music education) my own knowledge of music is quite bad. I was quite ashamed of this, so I have tried to improve my knowledge of music by going to concerts and buying classical CDs. I must say, though, that pop music holds a big place in my heart, so, if I had to chose between the music of Brahms, which I love, and Biagio Antonacci, I would go for the latter.

Now, the 10,000-euro question is: will classical and operatic music ever come back into fashion in Italy? It's not impossible: younger performers are now attracting a young audience: Andrea Bocelli, as previously mentioned, is a prime example, but there's also Cecilia Bartoli and Alessandro Safina, and surely Ludovico Einaudi, the world-famous composer and pianist who is well-known for his work on theatrical productions, are contributing in a major way to this revival. Also, the mixture of genres has made classical and operatic music accessible to larger audiences, and the recent success of musicals in Italy proves that there is a lot going for all genres at present.

Writing for the stage and for musicals seems to be a new interest for some famous Italian pop artists like Riccardo Cocciante and Lucio Dalla, and all this is contributing to a new attitude to classical music.

Let's hope the state will give more grants to improve music centres and the teaching of classical music in schools, so that the Land of Music will return to its former glory, and perhaps produce new Italian music geniuses, the likes of whom we haven't had for some time now.

I'm certain that such a revival would be a natural consequence of the musical soul that all Italians have. Knowing Italy and our lifestyle also means embracing our love for music, passion, beauty and harmony. Music is one of our favourite topics of discussion and the big summer festivals in many parts of Italy have an impact on all of us.

Since the 'nineties, in fact, summertime has again become the time for listening to and playing music: thanks to our long balmy evenings in July and August, nearly every village and town has a music festival or a cycle of concerts in the open air of a piazza or garden. Classical music and opera, along with traditional folk songs, Neapolitan songs, *sceneggiate*, *stornelli* and many other forms of traditional music express a lot about us. And it's not just fashionable to go to concerts, it's a way to connect with friends, loved ones and family and to pay homage to the beauty of the land which has always been associated with *bel canto* and with musical creativity of a very high standard.

Music is connected to theatre as well, naturally, and Italy, with its carnival parties and Goldoni theatre masterpieces, is the ideal place for new, unusual musical genres to emerge. *Canto carnascialesco*, carnival song, was the title of a poem by Lorenzo il Magnifico, and during the Renaissance these carnival songs were very popular in the centre of Italy. Other examples of how the joy of life is so connected to music and has always been inspiring wonderful Italian creations are *Canto Gregoriano*, as a hymn to religion, *Ballata* as a dance and song for a loved person. Even our modern pop singers, with all their various styles – from rap to love songs, from rock to *melodico* (a pop style similar to the traditional ballads created in the UK during the 'eighties) – often have remarkable personalities and use their music not only to celebrate life but also to describe our land and its beauties and troubles. Love songs are possibly the only genre in Italy that is more popular than the self-referential song. In fact, from 'L'*Italiano*' by Toto Cutugno to '*Viva l'Italia*' by De Gregori, Italy and the amazing stories of its people and places have been among the favourite themes of our songwriters, from opera to the popular *canzonetta*, (small happy song).

12. Cinema and Television: The Golden Era, The Veline Era and Beyond

'We all need illusions. That's why we love movies'

– Monica Bellucci

ITALIAN CINEMA AND TV: EXCELLENCE, FAME, NUDITY, past glory and present struggle, big names and starlets who want to hit the big time by showing their cleavage. Like politics and sports, this is the field where our contradictions emerge the most, making Italy a country that never goes unnoticed.

It's somehow clear to everybody that our cinema is not what it once was. You can't repeat films like De Sica's or Fellini's, you're not necessarily going to find actors like Marcello Mastroianni or Gina Lollobrigida among the current New Wave of our films. The magic, as we once knew it, may be lost but a new era has begun, and many positive signals are coming from new actors and directors since the 'nineties. Giuseppe Tornatore's *Nuovo Cinema Paradiso* marked something of a rebirth of our great screen productions, together with Salvatores's *Mediterraneo*, and relatively new names like Nanni Moretti have been able to bring a breath of fresh air to our cinema.

The birth of many Italian Film Festivals around the globe shows that the popularity of our cinema is again on the rise, and the international success of directors like Muccino, who is working in the USA (*The Pursuit of Happyness*), and actors like Monica Bellucci (*The Matrix*) and Caterina Murino (007 *Casino Royale*) is a good sign for our film industry.

But of course *Cinecittà è lontana*: the days of *Cinecittà* are long gone as the papers usually say – meaning that the Golden era of our cinema is now finished. But *Cinecittà*, the amazing City of Films in Rome, founded by Mussolini in the 'thirties, is still the most well-equipped area of Europe for film-making: with impressive facilities, everything from production to editing to special effects takes place in this amazing place, spreading over 400,000 square metres not far from Rome. Three thousand films have been made here, 82 of them nominated for Oscars with 47 actually winning.

Many masterpieces have been made there, from *Quo Vadis* to *Ben Hur*, *Cleopatra* to *The Name of the Rose* and *The Godfather* III, from *La Dolce Vita* to internationally successful films by Martin Scorsese such as *Gangs of New York*.

Its heyday was in the 'fifties, and now, after a period when it was mainly a monument to the past glories of Italian cinema, *Cinecittà* is again *the* place for making films, with a huge number of soundstages, props, special effect facilities and a digital division where many great digital productions are made every year.

Italian cinema is now growing again, with new filmmakers bringing a lot of prestige to our big screens. With them, have come a new crop of creatives, set designers, costume makers, prop creators, etc; this year's Oscar for Best Art Direction was won by two Italians, Dante Ferretti and Francesca Lo Schiavo for the film *Sweeney Todd* starring Johnny Depp.

Our cinema is not dead: our film and TV productions are not just cheap trash made with starlets who can't act: we have actors and actresses that are once again famous all over the world, and film directors who can still gain international recognition.

We may not currently have a new Fellini, Antonioni or Rossellini, of course; and the 'seventies and 'eighties was not a particularly groundbreaking period for Italian cinema, notwithstanding masters like Lina Vertmüller or Antonioni himself. But it wasn't easy to keep up with the works of De Sica and De Santis and their contemporaries – the Italian Neorealism cinematic movement in the post-Second World War period was one of the greatest ever achievements of world cinema.

Italy has a lot to offer international cinema once more: we have some great actors and a few Italian films have won Oscars in recent decades. The charm and atmosphere that our cinema had in the 'fifties and 'sixties will probably never be exactly repeated, but like all art forms, cinema has evolved, and it's certainly not the case that our greatest films are behind us.

On the small screen times have also changed and making it big in TV has replaced cinema in the dreams of many people, however, our TV is not among the best in the world!

Press articles and gossip magazines sometimes describe the world of Italian showbiz as a mixture of cheap porn and large breasts, but in amongst this we have some really good productions that are shown at new festivals, as well as at Cannes, Venice and more.

Author Adrian Michaels argues that in Italian culture there is a connection between nudity, chauvinism and a lack of professional success for women. So, while the classic 'mamma' is in the kitchen making pasta, her daughters dream of becoming successful just by being young and beautiful. Also, the author seems to believe that there is a link between the higher success of men in the workplace and the way women are presented through advertising. The same paper argues that women's image is exploited to sell products and that feminism is basically dead in Italy. But this is simplistic: we have to make a distinction here.

Of course we have ambitious teenagers who want to become actresses or showgirls, and whose only dream is to appear on the cover of B*ella* or G*razia* as top model or to win a beauty contest. Of course we have programmes like S*triscia la Notizia* (shown on Canale 5), which features girls (*veline*) wearing little in the way of clothing. This type of programme is popular, so it continues to be produced. Audience figures are important in Italy, as elsewhere; a programme that doesn't have enough viewers will be scrapped in no time from our channels. So it would be enough to turn the TV off when they show half-naked girls, but people don't do this.

Thousands of girls who want to be *veline* queue outside the Canale 5 studios during the selections, but then thousands of girls do the same for British and American B*ig Brother* castings. We should not think that Italian girls are the only ones wanting to become famous in this way: once it was cinema, now the hunger for fame via appearing on TV is a global phenomenon.

But our young people have other ambitions as well: the high numbers of female students in our universities show how much we believe that academic achievement is the basis for success in the world. An increasing percentage of young people – both boys and girls – want to become famous in showbusiness. But then, it's always been like this. A very famous film by Luchino Visconti, *Bellissima*, with Anna Magnani, (1951) tells the story of a mother who becomes obsessed with her small daughter becoming famous at any cost.

We may always be criticised for not condemning nudity on TV – what I said about Italians liking sexy clothes even in the workplace is valid here too: our love of beauty and image does make us different from other cultures. It is also true that we don't find it degrading to show some cleavage on television, as long as it's good to look at, just like we don't find a tasteful compliment to our breasts or legs offensive in the least.

Female beauty, as many have observed, does occupy a central place in our society and in our cinema and TV, and, since feminism hasn't been as strong here as in other countries, beauty is often exploited in ways that can seem undermining to women.

The most striking phenomenon has been this 'universal' desire to appear on television, and it has become the realm of many people of different ages. In my own experience, I took part in two TV quizzes on general culture and I won the *Rai quiz L'eredità* in 2006. TV in Italy is a lot of fun, and, taking part in these programmes, I realised that the quality of our production is improving, that people who work in both the private networks and the national Rai channels are extremely professional, and that creativity is surely helping to create new, dynamic productions loved by different ages and cultural levels. Our television is really getting better.

Challenging, lively, intelligent programs are replacing the old offerings of quiz-hosted-by-bikini-clad-woman, and this new tendency is making those old-style programmes still shown on the privately owned networks look out of date and tasteless. A good sign.

In fact, our TV has never been all bad: we have informative, good journalism and lifestyle programmes that are very well made, travel and history programmes, and a lot of good TV series with brilliant actors, produced by RaiFiction, for example, that are sold all over the world.

Another function of TV in Italy in recent years has been satire, mainly political. It was TV that launched Beppe Grillo, a comic actor who was actually banned from being broadcast after a while, as he was fearless in how far he would go in talking about our scandals and our contradictions. Grillo continues to be a theatre actor, one of our most popular, and still campaigns against issues like corrupt politicians who are still in parliament and immunity for politicians. He has a large number of followers during these campaigns, and his blog is extremely popular. Other satirical programmes in the 'eighties and 'nineties had a lot of viewers, and other humour shows have a big fan base. Recently, for example, *Zelig* on Channel 5 and *Le Iene* on Rai TV has seen a revival of this genre, a favourite for people of all ages in Italy.

According to *The Financial Times*, for example, women on Italian TV are mainly used in light entertainment, as actors, singers and models, which was true until a few years ago. But today more and more news programmes and journalistic features are hosted by women: travel, cookery, sports, programmes about missing people, satirical shows, investigative journalism, educational and children's programmes are hosted by good women journalists. Although the best-selling productions on prime-time are still mostly hosted by men for the moment. But relatively new names like Antonella Clerici, who conducts a daily cookery programme similar to *Ready Steady Cook*, a good sports journalist, Ilaria d'Amico, who hosts the Formula 1 programmes on Rai, or Federica Sciarelli who conducts *Chi l'ha visto?*, with features on people who leave home and are sought by their families, are all really known and loved TV personalities who are very professional and don't show too much flesh.

Even in daytime TV Rai has managed to produce two quite interesting lunchtime programmes, on the Rai1 and Rai2 channels, one mostly about showbiz and music, the other focused on daily events and politics. Late-night TV is also very interesting and informative, with well-respected journalists hosting debates about important public figures: here, both on Canale 5's *Maurizio Costanzo Show* and on Rai 1's *Porta a Porta*, you can see our politicians debating their election programme or new laws proposed in Parliament.

So, although you'll still see some flesh on some of our TV shows, thankfully higher quality programmes are becoming the norm.

* * *

Although TV in Britain is different, I do have a certain admiration for the openness that we have in Italy about sex: when I arrived in the UK my husband pointed out to me that *The Sun* newspaper has a certain reputation because of the Page 3 photo. In Italy we of course have pornographic publications, but we don't have Page 3-style photos in our press. So if our children open a daily paper they won't find naked breasts all over it.

To tell the truth, in Italy we have a positive, healthy approach to sex and we would find a Page 3 quite ridiculous. We think it's better to show some healthy cleavages and some good buttocks on TV for the teenagers to see rather than encouraging an attitude towards sex as something taboo.

We have had sex on the screen and on sale for a long time (and we don't know what the 'watershed' is, frankly, although a system of symbols has been introduced to help people understand which programmes are suitable for children and which are not). And for a long time our favourite 'porn magazine' has starred Valentina, a beautifully drawn cartoon character by the cartoonist Crepax. She's sexy, smart and often naked, but the cartoons are not vulgar, in fact, they're really nice to look at.

But where are the origins of this part of Italian culture? Cinema has had played a big part in it, and it has always been extremely loved in my country. Cinema arrived shortly after the Lumière brothers' invention and was adopted almost immediately with enthusiasm. Rodolfo Valentino, possibly the first star of our cinema, was the symbol of our early films and was known all over the world both as an actor and a sex symbol, starring in important films like *The Sheikh*.

Surely though, the best years of our cinema were those between the 'forties and the 'sixties, when actors, filmmakers and scriptwriters produced amazing master-pieces. It wasn't about getting Oscars or going abroad: it was more a fact of being proud of our nation and showing we could create wonderful cinema that could make history and inspire dreams. And it was very much about enter-taining people: going to the cinema was a treat, every town or village had its own cinema hall and the magic of this medium was able to conquer people of all classes and ages in our country. It was also what you did on Sunday afternoon, a cultural moment, a meeting point. The same was true of the first televisions that arrived at the end of the 'fifties: everybody would meet up in those houses that had a TV set to watch things like the Sanremo Music festival or the Giro d'Italia.

In 1962, my father, who had caught a first, brief sight of my mother while she was visiting some friends, and admired her long curly black hair, tried to find her again in the following days, in the village; the first place he looked for her was the cinema. But it was dark and she had her hair up so he didn't recognise her. Next thing he did, when he heard that my family's house had the first TV in the village and that people usually met there to watch it, was knock on our door and ask if he could watch the Sanremo Festival with everyone else … and it was there that he happily found my mother and talked to her for the first time.

So the importance of cinema and TV in Italy, during the economic boom, was certainly, again, this social side. It's undeniable that our films were among the best in the world in those decades. Between the 'forties and the 'sixties we had movements like Neorealism and Spaghetti Western which influenced cinema history worldwide. Films like *Bicycle Thieves* or *Sciuscià* by Vittorio De Sica, *Il Sorpasso* by Dino Risi, *I soliti ignoti* by Mario Monicelli, or *For a Fistful of Dollars* by Sergio Leone, *Blow Up* by Antonioni plus all the films by Pier Paolo Pasolini, are iconic and represent cult movies in their own right. A large number of actors and filmmakers were active in those decades, and even what we call Pink Neorealism, which launched actresses like Sophia Loren, Anna Magnani, Gina Lollobrigida, Silvana Pampanini, Lucia Bosè, Claudia Cardinale, and actors like Ugo Tognazzi, Walter Chiari and Marcello Mastroianni, created a series of masterpieces starting with *Divorce, Italian Style* (1961).

Italian comedy was also born in the Fifties, and De Filippo

and Totò became famous, mainly in Italy, during this time. Names like musician Ennio Morricone and screenwriter Cesare Zavattini, together with directors like Rossellini, Visconti, Monicelli, Antonioni, Fellini and our greatest actors made Italian cinema great everywhere.

The 'eighties saw a big crisis in our cinema, and people questioned if Italian film would ever be able to surface again and be as great as it was. But thankfully it did.

At the beginning of the 'nineties, thanks mainly to Gabriele Salvatores and Giuseppe Tornatore, we did indeed succeed at the Oscars again, as did Roberto Benigni with *Life is Beautiful* some years later. People like Nanni Moretti, Marco Bellocchio, Gigi Amelio, Paolo Sorrentino, Paolo Muccino, Ferzan Ozpetek, Sergio Castellitto, Mimmo Calopresti, Carlo Verdone and Paolo Virzi *are* our new cinema, and we also have plenty of young actors like Margherita Buy, Castellitto himself, Giovanna Mezzogiorno, Caterina Murino, Silvio Orlando, Diego Abatantuono and possibly the two best-known Italian actors abroad: Roberto Benigni, who for thirty years has been our most famous and loved comic actor, and Monica Bellucci, now the epitome of modern Italian beauty.

Panorama, on 3 January 2007, gave ample space to this new 'exportable' Italian cinema, especially with regard to new Italian actresses who are now known around the world. But together with these new names, and with Carla Bruni, who features on the cover as the Italian who made the French president fall in love, the authoritative magazine also ends its article with an interview with Maria Grazia Cucinotta, who featured in a James Bond film as well as in one of the best-known films of recent years, *Il Postino* with Massimo Troisi. Cucinotta, a dark, Mediterranean beauty from Sicily, states with no hesitation: 'But Sophia is incomparable'.

Sophia Loren is still the symbol of Italian cinema, and of

Italian beauty. Cucinotta describes her as the Icon of Italian Cinema. Also, she adds something quite important to understanding again the different way in which we look at things in Italy: while in other countries femininity has perhaps been flattened by a different approach to life, women here have retained, and prioritised, their femininity in all aspects of their lives.

Interestingly, for a famous actress like Maria Grazia, it's considered negative to be 'like a male' if you are a working woman. You can read between the lines that our way of considering women in business doesn't have much to do with that of the rest of the world. And it's not a sign of being backward-thinking or less feminist than other women: it's simply the way we are, and we are proud of being different. That is probably why men – foreign men as well as the Italians – find us irresistible … on screen and in real life! (As discussed in The Rules of Attraction chapter.)

If you are intrigued by Italian cinema and would like to know more, and discover not only the classics of our beautiful movie production, but also the emerging talents, here is a brief guide to the best films available in the English-speaking world. Starting from one of the most loved genres, Romantic comedy. Italian cinema can offer a lot of good titles: beautiful films with great love stories, humour and brilliant acting.

A classic of the 'fifties is *Bread, Love and Dreams*, with the great Gina Lollobrigida, directed by Comencini is a good start. Progressing to the 'seventies, Lina Wertmüller made a few unmissable titles, like *Seven Beauties* with the great Giancarlo Giannini, and more recently *Ciao professore*, with Paolo Villaggio. Most recently, the young Gabriele Muccino has offered a couple of good titles, *The Last Kiss* and *Dictionary of Love*, and in fact he has even been working in the US with actors like Will Smith (*The Pursuit of Happyness*). Another great romantic comedy with a bittersweet aftertaste is *Bread and Tulips* by Silvio Soldini. In the same genre there are classics like *Il Postino* with Cuccinotta, by Massimo Troisi, *Marriage Italian Style* with Sophia Loren (by Vittorio de Sica), and *Respiro*, by E. Crialese, one of my favourite films ever.

As for films with drama and passion, Italian cinema naturally has quite a few, the most loved being *The Leopard* by Luchino Visconti, *Life is Beautiful* by Roberto Benigni and *Cinema Paradiso* by Giuseppe Tornatore. Other good titles in this popular genre are *Swept Away* by Lina Wertmüller and, more recently, *The Son's Room*, by Stefano Accorsi. If you like mystery or horror films, there is a classic by our loved horror moviemaker Dario Argento, *The Bird with the Crystal Plumage*, and the recent *I am not Scared*, by Gabriele Salvatores.

Mafia films of course are a classic Italian film genre, some of the must-see titles are *La Scorta* by Ricky Tognazzi, and the classic Visconti film *Rocco e I suoi fratelli*, with the fantastic Alain Delon.

There are many treasures to be found in the Spaghetti Western genre, but possibly the best is *My Name is Nobody*, by Sergio Leone, the creator of many great films like *For a Fistful of Dollars*, another classic of this unusual style.

If you are looking for unusual films difficult to place in a genre, you should not miss *L'avventura* and *Blow up*, by Michelangelo Antonioni, and Fellini films like 8 1/2, *Nights of Cabiria*, *Amarcord* and *La Strada*. But possibly the best ever Italian film that actually created the Neorealism movement and which delivers so much poetry and art in only a couple of hours' viewing is Vittorio de Sica's *Bicycle Thieves*; a masterpiece not to be missed.

13. Italy and Fashion: How Style Cannot Be Taught

'Fashion and Italy are synonyms'

(Zandra Rhodes)

A FEW YEARS AGO I HAD THE PRIVILEGE TO INTERVIEW the hugely popular British designer Zandra Rhodes, who had just launched the Fashion and Textile Museum in Bermondsey, London. She received the photographer and me in her atelier, which at the time was an amazing place overlooking London, filled with many unusual designer objects, clothes, and huge Z-shaped seats, glass ornaments and so on. The interview was followed by a visit to the Museum where Italian fashion has, of course been allocated a huge space. Rhodes said 'without Italy fashion wouldn't be what it is now'.

Try to imagine fashion as a huge FaceBook-style website where instead of people you have dresses and accessories. If you removed all the designers like Armani, Versace, Dolce & Gabbana, Valentino, Prada, Gucci, Fendi, Missoni, Max

Mara, Krizia, Cavalli, then what would be left? And what would the history of dressmaking, accessories and tailoring be without Capucci or Ferragamo, without the Fontana Sisters or Elsa Schiaparelli? It would be just like art without Leonardo or Michelangelo, or music without Verdi or Vivaldi, or literature without Dante or Boccaccio: a fragmented puzzle with many pieces missing.

Fashion as it is now – a booming industry in Italy, and one that can still adopt the mark 'Made in Italy' with pride – is the natural evolution of our great tradition of clothes-making. For centuries Italy was ahead in men's tailoring and generally a world leader in the quality of fabric and design: our reputation is possibly second only to France's, and goes back many, many years. In many Italian regions the textile industry contributes significantly to the economy. Also, Italy is the place for leather, jewellery, accessories; pieces that have been considered the epitome of luxury for a long time.

For 6 years the *Salone Internazionale del Lusso* in Vicenza has been attracting buyers and admirers from all over the world: only here can you buy a new model Ferrari, a diamond-studded pair of jeans or a jewel for hundreds of thousands of euros. But it's also the perfect place to see how much fashion and creativity in Italy are still among the best symbols of our country. And at the core of all of this there is the ethos of 'work', genius, good business sense and the will to create masterpieces of tailoring that dates back a long time.

My grandmother was a tailor for many decades. She also created beautiful women's dresses and ran a tailoring school in her home where she taught designing, dress-making and tailoring. She was also an agent for Singer and she went all over Siena and the south of the province, often on her bicycle, selling their lovely sewing machines.

She studied for her job at the end of the 'twenties, when the first names of Italian fashion started to become known all over the world. She was working and designing until the 'eighties, so I grew up in a household where the men would go into the fields at dawn to care for the olives and vines and the women would sometimes never go to bed as they were too busy sewing a dress for a party or finishing a suit. The people who used to live in the farm facing our house would ask my grandmother if she ever slept. 'We go to bed and your light is on, we get up and your light is on…', they used to say to her.

My grandmother was very proud of having designed and created for many important clients – the crème de la crème of Tuscany and also the Schoenberg counts in Germany. A friend of Sorelle Fontana who was living in the village asked her if she wanted to meet them, as she had all the necessary skills and qualities to work with them in their Rome atelier. But my mother was a little girl at the time and my grandmother turned down the offer because she didn't really want to miss the best part of her daughter's childhood. But she was ambitious, and I don't think she ever forgot missing that chance. However, the fact of her having been offered it was proof of her qualities as a professional with talent and creativity.

I grew up surrounded by beautiful fabrics and lovely designs, and by the time I was six or seven I started to appreciate the high quality of the things my grandmother made for me. Later, as a twenty-year-old, I used to draw things and she would then make them for me, like a beautiful brocade two-piece evening dress in green and silver which I still have, and a wonderful pure wool white coat that she made for me in 1992 that I still wear.

She had many stories to tell. My favourite one was about

the Second World War, when a German general with a few of his soldiers were told my grandmother made uniforms, so they turned up on our doorstep and asked her to redo their uniforms in a hurry.

My grandmother was naturally frightened at first: this was the time when two men of the village were shot dead by the Germans for not obeying their orders. But the soldiers spoke to her in Italian and were very kind, so she worked and worked and made a whole new wardrobe, 'and trousers with lots of pockets', for them before they left again. I think it was a good experience: the young soldiers showed her photos of their families in Germany and made friends with her (while my mother and all our female relatives were hiding in the shelter up in our vineyard). My grandfather would come back from work and see that everything was fine: he knew my grandmother was a very strong person and didn't let anybody walk over her. Also, there was a strong network of neighbours around who would look after each other.

Our summer Tuscan travels were great: one place where she would go to work was the beautiful Villa di Pratolino near Florence. She also later worked at the Ospedale Militare San Gallo, a military hospital in Florence, where she used to sew the habits for the nuns and the soldiers' uniforms. I thought that her job was great: creating dresses for important people, and I remember dreaming of doing the same.

Those in fact were the years when the ancient tradition of dressmaking was starting to become real *prêt-à-porter* design and, in fact, art. The sort we admire in large exhibitions all over the world dedicated to our greatest fashion designers, from Versace to Armani, in museums all over Italy such as the *Galleria del Costume* in Florence, *Civiche Raccolte d'Arte applicata* in Milan, *Museo di Palazzo Fortuny* in Venice, and many more.

Between the end of the nineteenth century and the 'fifties a huge number of people were working in dressmaking in Italy. Many workshops sprung up in every town and village, and little by little it developed into an important industry.

Innovation was already central to Italian fashion at the beginning of 1900. Perhaps not everybody knows of Elsa Schiaparelli who invented the backless swimsuit, the wraparound dress and the built in bra, for example: she, like Roberto Capucci and Sorelle Fontana came out of the same world my grandmother introduced me to.

It was an age when everybody wanted the perfect suit or evening dress, and it had to be unique, so the natural thing to do was go to the best workshop in town.

Of course this tradition was inevitable in a country where beauty and taste are strong national characteristics, and, for fashion as for many other things, art was already entwined very closely with creativity. An artist like Giacomo Balla, born in 1871, created paintings (and clothes) that were strictly connected to the Futurist movement, to the idea of speed and motors. He also wrote Il *manifesto futurista del vestito da uomo* (*The Futurist Manifesto for the man's suit*). He said that a man's suit should not have 'all neutral colours, nice, pale, patterns, … dot patterns … symmetry of cut.' A few years later, in 1920, Volt (Vincenzo Fani) published a '*Manifesto della Moda femminile*' (*Manifesto of Female Fashion*), where extravagance and cheap materials were considered the best, and where he suggests the use of rubber, paper, foil … fish skin!

Milan and Turin's Esposizioni Universali at the beginning of last century further reinforced the connection between art and fashion, and little by little the couturier was becoming a fashion designer, and the designer was making clothes for everybody and not only for the rich. Next step: the department store.

In Italy the first department stores were opened in 1917, La Rinascente, (a name suggested by the writer and poet Gabriele d'Annunzio) and in 1919 Upim was born in Milan. Both these are still very popular now for clothes, and at the time they introduced a whole new universe for shoppers and for designers, who could show their *prêt-à-porter* fashion at a single price all over our country.

But it was, again, fascism which somehow promoted the birth of 'Made in Italy'. The fascist regime commissioned a survey in 1931 about fashion and clothing in Italy. From the survey it became evident that we were importing a huge amount of fashion from France, still the world leader in this sector. So, in 1932, a law was approved which allocated two million liras (a huge amount of money) for the building of the Ente Autonomo per la Mostra Permanente Nazionale della Moda, which became in 1935 L'Ente Nazionale della Moda. All aspects of our fashion industry went through this institution, and, ultimately, this started the Made in Italy as we know it now, although already in 1872 a 'Società Italiana per l'emancipazione delle mode' was founded as a reply to French supremacy in fashion.

Nationalism was very strong from the end of the nineteenth century to the First World War and Fascism's message promoted the qualities of Italy and the fact that our production was supposed to be coming out of a reborn country.

It goes without saying that the dictatorship had very many negative sides, but not for fashion, which, all through the 'forties and 'fifties, (and thanks to Rome being a jet-set city for film stars), was going through a golden era.

Sofia Gnoli, the author of a beautiful book on the history of Italian fashion (Un secolo di moda italiana, Molteni published in 2005) places the birth (or re-birth) of Italian fashion in the year 1951, when Giovanni Battista Giorgini founded the *Sala Bianca di Palazzo Pitti* in Florence, an institution at which all great designers dream of showing their creations. Florence became the centre of fashion for Europe and for the world after this point, and it still offers the chance to those interested in fashion to study and develop their skills. The city's *Accademia Italiana* for fashion designers is one of the most renowned in this field.

After all this is the town of Emilio Pucci, Salvatore Ferragamo, Gucci and of Pitti Uomo, Pitti Bimbo, Pitti Filati; very important appointments on the global fashion calendar.

Italy's other fashion city is of course Milan which will be the location for the *Città della moda*, an incredible project to be completed by 2010, and which will cost 680 million euro. It will be a 'town within the town': a series of amazing buildings all dedicated to fashion as a business, as a phenomenon; fashion as success and creativity and art. Fashion shows, museums, retail spaces, offices, showrooms, places to encounter the soul of modern fashion and other modes of design such as furniture, it will also host an ambitious architectural project including a building which will be 150 metres tall.

In fact, from 1990 to today Italian fashion has seen a tendency to borrow from architecture, sports, the media: and this sort of thing is what appears on TV, in the reality shows and in fashion magazines. But the classy, unmistakable mark of the great designers is still highly visible: after 2004 and 2005, when Made in Italy was showing a relative crisis in income, the latest years have shown a recovery: the end of 2006 marked a growth of over seven per cent, instilling a new confidence in all those involved in related industries. In particular, Italian accessories are the most sought-after in the world: according to the Italian trade website, (www.italtrade.com), our jewellery sector grew fourteen per cent during 2007, with a surprising amount being bought by the Chinese and Japanese. The best leather goods and luxury footwear come from Italy and world market-share grows every year. Also, an amazing twenty-seven per cent of the world's eyewear comes from Italy (with seventy per cent of luxury glasses coming from our country!). There's also our millinery: Italy produces wonderful hats, and the well-known brand Borsalino, made famous by Humphrey Bogart and Alain Delon, was in fact invented here 150 years ago.

Today, although there's a noticeable exchange of talent between Italy and other countries, for example Tom Ford for Gucci, there's no doubt that the best names in world fashion are still Italian. Our modern designers celebrate their classic heritage: famous names like Elsa Schiaparelli, who worked with Salvador Dalì, has had an Armani collection dedicated to her. And then of course there is fusion, ethnic influences, geometric and retro, vintage and futurism. Italian fashion does not go unnoticed: it is still made by an avantgarde group of artists and creative people who give a unique touch to their creations. Our creativity, skill and originality, energy and passion for detail are trademarks of a realm where we have been, for many decades, absolute leaders.

Italy is central in the world of fashion not only because of its creatives and designers, and for the quality of materials like textiles, but also for a great number of fashion photographers. *The Big Book of Fashion*, a global fashion directory, includes over sixty Italian designers, a few Italian models and great photographers like Oliviero Toscani. G. Paolo Barbieri, Fabrizio Ferri, F. Scavullo: their work is yet another example of the inherent Italian love of beauty and the good things in life, which naturally leads to creativity and imagination.

The secret of our success can be found in the extreme elegance and originality of our clothes and accessories: but also, somehow in the fact that Italian fashion doesn't just dress the elegant woman, our designers also think about the woman on the street, and about those who are not exactly conventional beauties. Once the great designer Gianni Versace said that while other designers create for princesses and beautiful women, he designed for sluts, something that says a lot about our fashion. Women come in all shapes and sizes, and they are sometimes designed on the Madonna model, sometimes on the Whore model. Italian fashion caters for both!

Versace also preached the individuality factor as one of the most important when it comes to dressing. I think his statement summarises well the spirit of Italian fashion:

'That is the key of this collection: being yourself. Don't be into trends. Don't make fashion own you, but you decide what you are and what you want to express by the way you dress and the way you live.'

14. Design and Architecture: Beauty is Truth, Truth is Beauty

'La nuova Fiat 500 appartiene a tutti noi' (The new Fiat 500 belongs to all of us)

– From a 2007 advertisement for the New Fiat 500

THE CINQUECENTO CAR, OF ALL THE CARS FIAT HAS designed, is possibly considered the one that best represents the Italian dream and its connotations. Small, sleek, agile; the classic Cinquecento was voted *Top Gear*'s sexiest car in the world. You can't beat its design and popularity: the Italians' fascination for it dates back to the end of the 'fifties and, with its new model launched in 2007, the European Car of the Year 2008 is once again a bestseller in many countries.

The natural interest Italians have always shown in engine design and vehicle production has resulted in a large number of enormously desirable cars, and global success. But Italy has also created two small jewels frequently associated with us: the Fiat 500 and the Vespa. These are small, affordable miracles of our design, and, if Ferrari is a status symbol, then Cinquecento and Vespa are our signature: they are the way Italians have travelled around since the 'fifties; the epitome of classy agility.

Both of these creations represented the *boom economico* of the 'sixties. After the war, Italy became an economic power, and people could afford to live in towns, and to have holidays in the summer during August. Convoys of 500s would leave the towns heading for the *Riviera Adriatica* or the lakes. The Cinquecento was the first car for many people born in the 'forties, and my father, for one, was a great lover of them. I have two 500s, and many of my friends would love to buy them, but they can dream on!

Vespa, on the other hand, became world-famous after the film *Roman Holiday*, and its popularity never really diminished. In London now you can find hundreds of them parked in fashionable areas: it's possibly still the most popular scooter amoung the young and old alike.

* * *

Architecture and design are part of the backbone of Italy: these aspects of our country have inspired many travellers to visit and often fall in love with this incredible place.

The world of architecture and design wouldn't be the same without Palladio, Bernini or Brunelleschi; without the Vespa scooter or the Olivetti typewriter. Beauty of line, harmony of space and colour, the quest for perfection and elegance of form are at the basis of these creations. No matter if the aim is designing a villa in Veneto or a new *caffettiera*: what counts is achieving this aesthetic balance that turns a functional item into an *objet d'art*.

During the various *esposizioni internazionali* (international exhibitions) at the end of the eighteenth and beginning of the nineteenth century, in Paris and in Italy, our design creations were indeed the most admired, but there is no doubt that the best examples of these designs are in our streets, in our small and large towns, in all those corners where unexpected buildings, churches, houses and squares are constant reminders of the superiority of our architects over most of the rest of the world.

After all, as Jeremy Clarkson put it, the passion for aesthetics that exists in Italy cannot be found anywhere else.

In *The Story of Western Architecture* by Bill Risebero, Italy, Italian monuments and Italian architects appear in the index with a frequency of one in every four (the book covers all continents of the world from classical period to the present). It also fixes the origins of basilica, of classical styles and of modern architecture in Roman times and gives a precise, detailed list of civil and religious places in Italy that have taught important lessons to the world.

Starting from the ancient Mediterranean populations, through to Greek and Roman times, the author looks at beautiful buildings like the Colosseum, the Palladium, the Roman forums, early basilicas, towns like Pompeii, works like paved roads and baths, houses with under-floor heating, aqueducts and theatres. All of these monuments to ingenuity are still visible now, having survived for more than two thousand years. Roman architects were clearly vastly ahead of their time: using their skills, originality and creativity they introduced many elements of design and functionality that are still in use today. To mention but one of their creations, the Flavian Amphitheatre, or Colosseum, was evidently built to last: innovative materials like lava in the foundations and tufa in the arches were used, guaranteeing the strength of the structure, so that we are still able to sit in the Colosseum today.

The Great Empire also meant that many of these building techniques were taken overseas. In many colonies including Africa, the Middle East, Gallia, Great Britain, so many countries had the benefit of the Romans' skills in this rich tradition and of their will to share it with many other people.

From Roman times all through the Middle Ages and the Renaissance, Italy has been leading in the art of designing and building for the Church and for the people. Our towns speak for themselves. In fact, thanks to the respect that the Italians have always had for art, history and beauty, Italy has kept intact many of these works from the past, and, from North to South to the islands, Italy contains 47 World Heritage sites protected by Unesco. From small towns like Ferrara or Padova to the great cathedrals of Milan and Siena, from the first town ever built as an application of a humanist planning concept (Pienza, South of Siena), to monasteries, squares, towers and whole villages, our architecture is possibly the most photographed and studied in the world. But why is this?

The presence of the Pope in Vatican City, of a large 'army' of bishops and cardinals, and the 'competition' between the Pope and the secular power that went on for centuries after the year 1000 were the central reasons for Italy becoming world-leaders in architecture.

The fact that huge monuments like St Peters were built is mostly thanks to the Church. However, a large number of lesser known monuments were conceived in the same way. My experience is that the will of the Church, and also its wealth, transformed even small places like mine. In fact, principally thanks to its beautiful hilly landscape, our territory was chosen by the Bishop of Siena as the site for his residence in the year 1151. Lupompesi, Crevole, Murlo, Montepescini and the rest of our castles and villages remained the Bishop's property until the eighteenth century. This meant that the Bishop managed, over the years, to build or improve many of the monuments, castles and churches we still admire now, his presence in the area also meant that great works of art (paintings and scultures) were commissioned for Murlo. Paintings by Duccio di Buoninsegna, Sano di Pietro, Ambrogio Lorenzetti, Benvenuto di Giovanni, were made for our churches, and the Bishop's palace in Murlo, now home of the Etruscan Museum, is possibly one of the most magnificent civil buildings in the province of Siena.

The tiny village of Murlo itself, enclosed within its fine red walls, overlooking an amazing landscape of wooded hills, is one of the most admired Medieval centres in Italy, only recently discovered by a discerning number of tourists.

Of course the Bishop, having money and power, wanted all the best things and managed to enclose them in a large and rich territory like ours. So, now in Vescovado we can still admire works of art like the incredible Polyptic by Benvenuto di Giovanni in the San Fortunato Church. And the Madonna di Crevole, now at the Siena Pinacotheque, by Duccio di Boninsegna, takes her name from the place where the artwork was found, one of the oldest castles still standing in the Siena province, Crevole.

Italy's being a collection of rich states over the Middle Ages and Renaissance, meant that an amazing amount of splendid buildings went up. The idea of commissioning large, important architectural masterpieces was the obvious way to demonstrate the importance of the Signore or Prince or Bishop who ruled that particular town or state. For example, almost all of Siena as we see it now was built during the Republic period, especially in the thirteenth and fourteenth centuries: Siena being independent and very powerful could afford to have important architects and builders, and the rich families had a sort of 'competition' going between them. The family who built the highest tower won. This 'phallic' idea of power involved the Church and the State as well: the Tower of the Townhall in Piazza del Campo (the famous Torre del Mangia) and that of the Siena Cathedral were built in a way that, from a distance, they could appear to be the same height, for that same principle. Of course architectural marvels like San Gimignano are what they are because of this duel for the highest tower: no other town in the world has as many towers, and this is what it makes it so unique. Another success of 'campanilism'.

Our traditions in this field go back many centuries. The presence of different populations in our regions through the years, from Arabs to Huns, from Greeks to Phoenicians, made possible the amazing variety of Italy's architectural heritage.

In Siena we are very lucky because we have examples of incredible achievements dating many centuries before Christ as well as examples of wonderful Medieval buildings.

Even places like Murlo show how architecture was a way to impress and inspire awe among the people in ancient times. Poggio Civitate, which I mentioned in the Food and Wine chapter, was the site where an important prince used to live. The Etruscans were a population possibly originated from Lydia, in what's now Turkey, who chose the centre of Italy as their new home after they left their land for some still unknown reason. The importance of the Etruscans lies in their amazingly advanced culture and sense of beauty and harmony; the paintings in tombs still present at Tarquinia, for example, show how much their love of life and pleasures inspired beautiful arts and their belief in life after death. The Romans learned a lot from them, especially from the Etruscan architects who built impressive palaces and homes.

The Etruscan prince in Murlo lived in a residence built seven hundred years before Christ that has been identified as very important for understanding Etruscan architecture. It had a very modern and efficient way of distributing water and of collecting rainwater from the roof, but also it had beautiful decorations all made locally of terracotta that stood on the roof and made the huge building a masterpiece.

A fire destroyed the palace which meant it had to be rebuilt. The resulting structure has been kept almost intact over time: the Etruscans in fact, before leaving their village for unknown reasons, decided to hide the palace without destroying it. So they took the building apart, piece by piece, and buried it in deep holes dug in the ground. When archaeologists found it in 1966, they were amazed to find all the terracotta decorations and all the functional parts of the building preserved underground. They were able to reconstruct this palace in the Museum: the statues that were found are impressive, especially because all of them were built in the village (they also found a workshop with clay and terracotta tiles and decorations), and they depict some unusual themes, particularly the famous 'Man with Cowboy Hat'. This is, for the scientists, possibly the Prince himself, sitting on a throne, wearing a large hat and a square beard, hands resting on his knees and his eyes surveying the landscape in front of him. Nothing similar has ever been found by archaeologists – it's a unique object of design, as are the frontal motifs that used to be all around the huge building. This discovery has told scientists a great deal about Etruscan architecture and has also confirmed the possibility that the Etruscans arrived from Turkey. Oriental influences can in fact be found in the Palace and in the site of Poggio Civitate, not least in the way the hollow terracotta statues were built.

The people of Murlo were impressed to know that this hill was chosen by such a population to be made into one of the important sites of ancient Etruria. In primary school our teacher used to take us to Poggio Civitate and also to the conferences that were organised to present the work the archaeologists were doing. It was all fascinating and exciting for us, and we grew up surrounded by the privilege of having such a treasure close-by as well as many other architectural jewels on our hills, like Medieval castles and monasteries.

This is another huge part of people's fascination with Italy: you don't have to be born in Rome, the Eternal City, or in Venice to be able to enjoy the richness of our art. A small place like Murlo, although not as famous or as flooded with tourists, is home to many marvels.

This tradition of architectural achievements didn't stop in Renaissance times. I could devote another book entirely to Risorgimento (the end of the nineteenth century), to the Fascist period – the *Casa del Fascio* by Giuseppe Terragni is one of the highlights of this period. For architecture, our colonialist ambition which took us to Africa, was also very important: Asmara has many beautiful Art Deco buildings designed and built by Italians that are much admired by the world.

Between Art Nouveau and Futurism, the names of Raimondo D'Oronoco and Antonio Sant'Elia were probably the greatest to emerge, but last century also saw a huge number of new creations in towns in the North, establishing, again, Milan as the capital of innovative contemporary architecture. This city has such a creative character to it that, in very recent years, every few months new things are being built: maybe just a shopping arcade or a new department store, but for sure things keep moving all the time in this incredibly industruous town.

So, if Turin and Genova have a treasure of cafés and beautiful little corners created in the nineteen-hundreds, Milan is in a continuous 'building mood', and the names of Gae Aulenti, Mario Bellini, Fabio Novembre, Massimiliano Fuksas, Antonio Citterio are only a few examples of the great talent involved.

In 2007 a book entitled *Design City Milan* was published in the UK. During a presentation by the author Cecilia Bolognesi at the Italian Cultural Institute, it was very interesting to hear the architect saying that this creative activity is always on the go. Bolognesi gave us an idea of how many buildings are currently being created in Milan and why the city is considered the World Capital of Design. She also explained that this New School of architects and designers is now contributing a lot to some new projects in London, bringing their creativity and originality to the new face of the UK's capital.

* * *

With no doubt the 'region of design' in Italy is Lombardy. Here, thousands of students from all over arrive every year to take up university courses taught by the greatest designers in the world. Design forms a great part of the enormous productivity of this region, which creates over twenty per cent of the PIL (*prodotto interno lordo*) of our economy. Not only Milan, but also smaller towns like Brescia are known for their creativity and the successful building of new small businesses and high-quality crafts are entwined very deeply in the output of this Italian region.

The continuing inventiveness in Italian architecture is noticeable in the examples of subsequent centuries, but I think that the importance of Italian design is possibly the logical product of this great inherent talent for working with shapes and volumes. The passion for working with line, for inventing new ideas of movement and of unusual dynamism that we Italians have takes the shape of innovation in everyday objects as well as in our motoring industry, which we'll look at in the next chapter.

Italian design is regarded as efficient, unusual, functional and original: even everyday things like Italian pepper mills are sold all over the world as an example of Made in Italy, and they are much more interesting than the same objects made in other countries.

Authoritative reference books like *History of Modern Design* by David Raizman, where the design of post-industrial revolution is analysed, puts Italy amongst the greatest creators of world design. If we start from the end of the nineteenth Century, we can see that the North of Italy, especially, is leading the international design forum, with the City of Turin being Italy's centre for design. It was in fact chosen for the International Exposition of Modern Decorative Art in 1902, even more amazing when we remember that Italy had only just been united, in 1861.

Italian design ingenuity took many forms, for example the chimneypiece manufactured by Vittorio Valabrega around the year 1900. This was made of walnut, brass and ceramic tile and was shown at the International Exhibition of Paris that year. Carlo Bugatti, father of car maker Ettore Bugatti, was another important designer of that period: he was original, genial and impressive in his use of creativity in furniture. He created the famous Snail Room shown at the Turin Exhibition, a masterpiece of curved lines and shiny metal pieces. His tables, chairs and benches used wood made into plastic curves and stretched shapes, covered with sheepskin and copper.

'Bugatti's designs are hardly derivative or historicist', writes Raizman, 'rather they exhibit a freedom from precedent and an inventiveness that informs much of the work treated so far ... namely the liberating effect of a closer relationship between fine art and craft.'

Futurism, a highly influential movement, began in Italy in 1909. Filippo Tommaso Marinetti, with his *Manifesto del Futurismo*, writes about the 'new beauty – the beauty of speed ... A roaring racing car, rattling along like a machine gun, is more beautiful than the winged victory of Samothrace'.

It's perhaps surprising to see an Italian write anything like this. It was shocking to realise that we could find more interest and aesthetical beauty in a motor car than in a classical work of art universally recognised. So the works by artists like Gino Severini and Giacomo Balla (as mentioned in the Fashion chapter) were most shocking for those Italians with more traditional sensibilities. This shift wasn't exclusive to arts and design: one of our greatest writers, Gabriele D'Annunzio, was sharing this passion for speed and noise and electricity and movement, and what Marinetti and Futurism did was to break away from the stabilility and classically oriented idea of art that filled our streets and squares and every corner of our cities.

Marinetti wanted to go beyond the idea of art in galleries or as monuments, to reach industrial workers in factories, people in the streets and in everyday environments. So writing was an important medium, seen as an image more than as mere means of expression, and generally art became more immediate, but also more intricate, so to speak. It was a revolution.

So, while cars and aeroplanes became essential for travelling, electricity became very important to the creative consciousness, as did the internal combustion engine; there was a new tendency to break free from the past, in many areas of culture and creativity. Raizman noted that this brought many new developments and new techniques in art, while freeing the artists from conventional methods of expression.

Art and design discovered collage, photography, fashion, geometrical shapes: between the First and Second World Wars a lot changed in Italian art and design, and the boom in what was fast, dynamic, agile, aggressive and also repetitive gave somehow a new twist to design for everyday objects. The advertising posters of that period are very interesting: Dinamo Azari, who created ads for great firms like Campari, was very influential with his angular shapes, cones, black-and-white prints and generally new ways of looking at and representing beauty and functionality.

The second big wave of innovation in Italian design was brought by the *boom economico* in the 'fifties and 'sixties. As mentioned, this was the time that the Vespa and the Fiat 500 were created to answer the new desire for easy travel. So, while society still struggled to get used to a new world where being on a farm was bad and being in a town was good (Italo Calvino says a lot about this in his seminal novel *Marcovaldo*), our designers found new motives to create. There was a very precise objective in the minds of Italian design, what Raizman calls 'conscious development of an international market and national image for Italian design in the post-war era'. A few Italian manufacturing companies had begun mass production after the First World War, and then the post-fascist era brought one of the eternal symbols of our design, Vespa. This was followed by a huge development of our car sales, which grew four hundred per cent between 1950 and 1961.

Among our finest creations of this period were Olivetti typewriters, designed by the famous painter and architect Marcello Nizzoli, bathroom accessories like the bathroom sink designed by Gio Ponti for Ideal Standard in 1953, and generally household products like lights and door handles. All this was happening because industrial manufacturing companies hired their own consultant designer in Italy after the war. These were important figures who had autonomy and influence, they were highly respected and valued, although they often created conflict within the companies they worked for. This tendency to work in an atmosphere of drama and conflict rather than hierarchical directive is what led to the creativity and dynamism that these companies became known for.

The Design Museum in London has many examples of Italian design, and its collections of chairs, furniture and household goods are rich in Italian names. Probably the most prominent name of recent decades is Achille Castiglioni, the architect, designer and tutor who launched the *Compasso d'Oro* prize at the celebrated *Triennale di Milano* (his own creations won this prize several years running).

Achille's students at the *Politecnico* remember him as an amazing tutor, always bringing new objects to his classes and showing students how they worked and how they were created. He had verve, personality, charm, and his lessons were exciting and really useful for all those who wanted to become designers too. So, here again it seems that the secret of success in this creative field is passion, of course, and an imaginative approach not just to design but to life generally – something, it seems, that is deeply embedded in our culture: the lightness of being, the *'simpatia'* and charisma that we have and want to share with others.

This approach to life is evident in the work our designers have done during the last century: one of the most famous examples is the Superleggera chair by the great designer and architect Gio Ponti: weighing only 1.7 kg, it can be lifted with one finger, thanks to its triangular shaped legs. Another piece of furniture that became famous for a second time after featuring on the reality show Big Brother in Britain in 2002 is the red Donna Up5 chair by Gaetano Pesce. Inspired by women's curves, the chair comprises a comfortable, soft scarlet seat with a ball as a separate cushion. This chair was designed by Pesce in 1969 as part of a collection of vacuum sealed furniture: when the vacuum seal was broken, the furniture would just spring to life and take its definitive shape.

The story of our design creations from 1861 to today has a very strong link with the Italian sense of beauty, and generally with our predilection with harmony and functionality all wrapped into perfect design.

The wonderful Italian imagination has taken various forms, and, since the beginning of the last century, we have led the way in design innovation. The winning ideas of Italian designers and architects have produced objects like 'the luminator' by Gio' Ponti: the first indirect light lamp to produce light by reflection, but also grand-scale projects like the Centre Georges Pompidou in Paris, created by Renzo Piano and Richard Rogers. It's possibly Renzo Piano who most represents our architectural ingenuity all over the world: he has worked with the greatest names in world architecture, such as Peter Rice, and he has conceived and built incredible works like the California Academy of Science in San Francisco, the *Parco della Musica* in Rome, the *New York Times* building and the Zentrum Paul Klee in Bern.

But what makes our design unique and so prestigious?

The answer can to be found in everyday objects that, for a small amount of money, bring the pleasure of owning something creative and special. Art in everyday life, perfection in action.

Let's look at one of the most interesting objects ever produced by our designers: the Arco lamp. In this amazing lighting creation there is somehow captured a whole world of creativity and style: the lamp, still in production since 1962, was created by the Castiglione brothers and it consists of a chrome ball shade, which is suspended seven feet from a marble base by a beautiful arch of steel. This idea was born out of a new concept, illuminating a room without having to make a hole in the ceiling. But then beauty and harmony and high style were added to this initial principle, making the Arco lamp one of the greatest symbols of our design. Many other examples can be added to this: everyday objects like light switches by Bticino or door handles by Olivari, and countless home appliances that made Italy the world's second largest exporter of such goods after the US.

Rationalism, post-modernism and many new styles were created in Italy, and now the *Compasso d'Oro* prize at the *Triennale* exhibition and the *Salone del Mobile* in Milan are among the most popular places in which to see the best design in the world.

From Corradino d'Ascanio's Vespa to Alessi kitchen accessories, the curvacious lines and the light, easy, functional way to interact with our daily life are symbolic. These objects are used and shown all over the world to represent Italy, perhaps as much as the images of our art in history books.

I was recently looking at a catalogue for storage solutions. My eye was caught by a collection of metal boxes that had Italian writing on them. One for memories, one for photos, one for *'da non buttare'* (things not to throw away), made of black and white tin and all with pretty little poems written on the sides. I immediately thought that they couldn't have been made in any other nation somehow, simply because we have a *'grande passione'* for simple, alluring lines precisely like these ones.

Some people say it's easy to excel in design when you are surrounded by beauty. In fact, art and history have a lot to do with the Italian creative flair: our Renaissance towns, such as Florence or Rome, say a lot about how our architects and designers managed to decorate and create beauty everywhere. The amazing painted ceilings of the Palazzo Vecchio, the *loggiati*, or arched parades, in many towns like Modena, Turin or Cagliari, The Doge's Palace in Venice, the gorgons our Etruscan architects used to decorate the fronts of palaces and private homes, the harmony of the interior courtyards in the town of Pompeii, which, in itself, exemplifies how much love and care was put into conceiving, designing and building a town in Roman times are just a few examples of how our architects, builders, decorators and designers have always had this great skill for creating beauty, even in unexpected places.

Surely, if our architecture is universally acclaimed and studied for its amazing qualities and innovation, our creativity and success in design is something harder to define. But there is no doubt that it has a lot to do with the Italian way of life, and with an airy, graceful, sensuous idea of harmony, Italian-style.

15. The Most Beautiful Cars in the World

'*Donne e motori gioie e dolori*' (*Women and motors –*
Joys and pains)

– Italian proverb

IT'S NOT BY CHANCE THAT WOMEN AND CARS ARE
often associated, as many Italian men find their love for cars
and engines comparable only to their love for women. Both,
though, are reason to suffer, of course: they are not always
reliable, they are temperamental but can be incredibly
beautiful. And of course, like Verdi wrote, they are both
extremely '*mobili*'.

As any wife or girlfriend can tell you, Italian men are
sometimes too fussy with their cars, and this can arouse
feelings of antagonism in some women. But, on the other
hand, it's not always the men's fault, since Italian motors are
traditionally so great. From Bugatti to Maserati, from Alfa
Romeo to Ferrari, from Ducati to Vespa, from Fiat to Aprilia,
Italian motoring creations have been widely acclaimed over

the years, not least because they have managed to win so many prizes and competitions, and they have featured in famous films and in all the world's media.

Michael Schumacher is universally recognised as the greatest racing driver of all time. He was World Champion seven times; nobody else has ever achieved that. Nobody thinks it's by chance that his record was achieved with Ferrari: a prestigious, reliable, great team, and in a car which has everything, from elegance to style, from speed to personality. Ferrari has won one in four Formula 1 Grand Prix races and has attained more pole positions than any other team since 1950, when the competition started. Ferraris have won the Constructors Championship fifteen times, they have won more than any other team: a legendary, literal track record that speaks of Italy all over the world.

The Galleria Ferrari is an incredible place, where the best design of the whole Formula 1 world, but also the main dream of many italians – owning a Ferrari – take the shape of a beautiful museum with class and style written all over it.

When I visited Maranello, which aside from Ferrari is the home of Maserati, it was pouring with rain, but I could still feel how much love there is in the place. Thousands of people in Emilia Romagna work for Ducati, Maserati and Ferrari, and they all talk about the place with great passion. They feel responsible for the safety of their creations, they feel proud to contribute to the brands' success: this is no ordinary job, and the ambitions of the young people here are not necessarily to become designers or engineers at Ferrari, but simple factory workers, so that they can feel part of the dream.

* * *

Red is the colour of passion and fire, and Ferrari. Red is also the colour of Ducati, a motorbike racing team that has also won everything in the competitions of recent years, becoming another legend for motorsports fans. The two Red Passions of Italy were both created in Emilia Romagna, a region of good food, good wine, where older people dance in competitions until they're ninety, where there is the greatest number of discos and bars in Italy.

Emilia Romagna is a creative place where you can eat *tagliatelle* while listening to a beautiful soft language that is, of course, Italian, but with something more sensuous, just a little bit more passionate than in other parts of the country. *Emiliano* and *romagnolo* accents sound a little like Spanish and a little like Greek, the women are soft and round and earthy, just like in a Fellini film: Fellini was indeed born here, and loved this amazing world of colours and invention. Fellini's Rimini has been for decades one of the top holiday destinations for people from all over Europe: Emilia Romagna's taste for the good life, and not just its sun and sea, is at the heart of the region's popularity. I don't think Ducati, Ferrari or Maserati could have been born anywhere else in the world.

Ferrari has millions of fans everywhere, and it is one of the symbols of Italian success in a time when the media tend to underline so many negative sides of our country. Just like when we won the World Cup in 2006, our national pride comes out again when we win the Formula 1 Grand Prix. The latest victory of 2007 was even sweeter since it was almost unexpected, and Raikonnen showed again how a great driver and a great car can together do wondrous things.

But Ferrari, seen as a status symbol and as a jewel of Italian design and technology, is only one example of how

Italy leads the world of motoring. Other names, like Alfa Romeo, Maserati, Lamborghini, and, in the 'twenties and 'thirties, the celebrated Bugatti, are all great examples of how creativity, skill, a sense of beauty and high-level engineering often come together in the Italians to create masterpieces in this field.

But our genius in this sector doesn't just take the shape of expensive, regal cars like these. Two small, iconic pieces of engineering and design have been representing Italy since the 'forties: the Vespa and the Fiat 500.

It was 1946 when Corradino d'Ascanio created the Vespa motor scooter by Piaggio. The Vespa was a stroke of genius: a small, practical, inexpensive way of getting around, a personal mode of transport with a streamlined body, ideal for driving in town as well as in the country. It took the place of bicycles, for those who could afford it, but mainly it became very soon the symbol of *'ricostruzione'*, of the rebirth of Italy after the war. 'The enclosure of mechanical parts, and the cutaway profile of the seat, introduced a graceful, sculptural element to the design, giving visible expression to an identification between freedom, democracy, and mobility in the Italian postwar ricostruzione', commented David Raizman in his *History of Design*. And the Vespa, which is now more and more, in large towns all over the world, a popular and elegant way of beating traffic with style, became at the time an instant icon of the Italian lifestyle, and took a special place in cinema history, after it starred, with Audrey Hepburn and Gregory Peck, in *Roman Holiday* (1949). The film wouldn't have been the same without this romantic, sleek scooter that carries the two protagonists to the most beautiful places of the Eternal City. A symbol of the Dolce Vita, of an easy, fun life in the sun, Vespa still appears in posters and advertising campaigns for Italian products, often together with another star of Italy's motor production that was created in 1955 by Dante Giacosa: the amazing Fiat 500.

The history of the Fiat 500, now recreated in a new model that's already topping the charts of car sales in Europe, is really interesting. It was crowned Sexiest Car in the World by *Top Gear* magazine, ahead of cars like the Aston Martin DBS and, of course, the Maserati Quattroporte in third place. According to the magazine's journalists, it emits pheromones from its tailpipe. James May added that 'it advertises nothing about its owner, except that it's someone who doesn't need to try'. This conclusion makes me very proud to be Italian, and it's significant to me as the car was part of the reason my husband fell in love with me when he first saw me: I was at the wheel of my fire-red 500. As I previously mentioned, I own two of them, a lobster-red 1972 Fiat 500 L, and a 1965 Fiat 500 D, both bought for me by my father whose passion for this car is well known among his friends and family.

It's a car which in the 'eighties was considered in Italy to be a relic from the 'fifties: now its status has been restored to that of an icon of our country, and it has achieved a prestige second to no other car. The 500 is famed for its practical, elegant, small bubble-like design that has been imitated without success many times by other car makers. The prototype of the 500 Topolino; the Zero A that would become the Fiat 500 in 1957, was in fact created by Dante Giacosa in 1934. The car that came out of this prototype was the first '*utilitaria*' Fiat, the 600, launched in 1955, which sold 2,600,000 units, a record for the time. When the Fiat 500 was finally launched on 4 July 1957, it wasn't love at first sight for the Italian audience. In fact it took a while before the new car became a favourite. That year Italy already had 25,000 km of state roads, ninety-five per cent of which were tarmacked, so driving was getting easier. The first motorway was to be opened one year later; it was the *Autostrada del Sole*, the Motorway of the Sun. With the new idea of the weekend as a two-day period when you could go out of town; with summer holidays becoming a habit for many families thanks to the economical 'boom'; and with women starting to have a voice in every choice of the family (starting to drive too, for example), the Fiat 500 was to become a must-have for many Italian families.

Of course many couldn't afford a car yet, so they chose Vespa instead, or Moto Guzzi, a very popular motorbike at the time. My mother and her cousin Mara were often taken to the seaside or into town by Mara's father Vasco, who had a Moto Guzzi and used to carry both of them on the back (no helmets, of course, and no health and safety concerns: it was still the time for carefree motorbike rides).

But then, when it came to selecting a car, of course the 500 was the obvious choice for a family, and this was the case up until 1975: the 500 R is was last one in the series, but after that year and almost 4 million cars sold, the Fiat 500 went from everyday object to legend. The fact that it won in 1959 the prize *compasso d'Oro* at the *Milano Triennale*, and that it was fast becoming an objet d'art, make 500 one of the most loved cars of all times.

Today it's the most stolen car in Italy, and the passion so many people have for the cars has preserved many of these little marvels. Italy has a number of 500 Fan clubs, and there are many meetings of 500s during the year. It got into the *Guinness Book of World Records* in 2006 for the longest Fiat 500 procession, two miles. The 500 starred in the Disney Pixar film *Cars* as Luigi, the 500 from Emilia Romagna whose dream is to meet a real Ferrari. The car has also appeared in many ads for beer, shoes, and for many other things where the Made in Italy trademark is important. Songs and poems have been dedicated to the 500, and many VIPs have been photographed driving them all over the world.

Among the most famous photos of this car, are the ones featuring Churchill and Onassis in Greece in a Fiat 500 Spider (1959), Jane Mansfied taken in 1957, Yul Brynner with his 500 Jolly-Ghia in 1964, and even one of the future Pope Paul VI at the presentation of the car in 1957. It might not be possible to own a Ferrari or a Maserati, but almost anyone can have the chance to be admired in the seat of a convertible 500 like mine. All my British relatives love it, and I have beautiful photos of me driving this car with my nephews Tom and Charles standing in it. At my wedding my husband and I were driven in my 500 to the restaurant: a wonderful, unusual wedding car!

Being voted European Car of the Year 2008 among 33 candidates, including Mercedes and Peugeot, by a very authoritative commission, for its charm, nostalgia, class, excellent features and design was a triumph for the Fiat 500 (www.caroftheyear.org).

The idea of recreating this car in 2007 was certainly a good one; it was also released with the intention of celebrating the fiftieth anniversary, and the new model retained some of the features that made it so famous. A new Fiat showroom was opened in January 2008 in London, and things are certainly looking up for our car industry. So, we are not just talking about old glories here, but about creativity that brings beautiful engineering to the motoring world. That passion that Italians have always had for cars and motorbikes, and even for scooters or motorboats (the Italian Riva Aquarama Speedboat was described by Jeremy Clarkson as the 'most beautiful man-made creation ever') is still creating success, and, judging from the lasting triumphs of Ferrari, this is not just a small part of our culture. Beauty, elegance, creativity and love are the foundations of our greatest achievements. Despite what you might read in the news.

16. Essere o Apparire? (Being or Appearing?): La Bella Figura, Arrangiarsi and How to Present Yourself ... Even in Politics

'Italy's history is also Europe's history ... Political changes elsewhere have often been experimented with in Italy, from euro-communism to the post-modern politics of Berlusconi ... Far from merely following other countries, Italy has often been a leader.'

– from Modern Italy by John Foot

VERY OFTEN ITALY AND ITS COMPLEX POLITICS APPEAR in the world's news. Italy has been considered a progressive country by some people, and a very backward nation by others. The characteristics of our politicians are original for sure: possibly nobody else has represented Italy, for good and bad, like our premier Silvio Berlusconi, with his flashy smile, classy clothes, dubious charm and shady past. An icon for Industrial Italy, he has overshadowed people like our great President of the Republic, Giorgio Napolitano, whom I met in London during his visit in 2006.

On that occasion, he gave a fantastic lecture at the London School of Economics, which I attended. He's a deeply sensitive and intelligent man with high cultural and moral sense who spoke in very good English in front of a crowded and interested auditorium about the role of Europe in the world, and about Italy and its place in Europe, covering interesting topics that kept the young audience alert and responsive.

Because Napolitano is seen as a 'good' symbol of our country, he's mentioned less by the media than Bad Bad Berlusconi; the cavalier Silvio has always managed to inspire the strongest reactions among my journalist colleagues. His contrasts and deficiencies make better news than a positive character like the President himself.

But there are other reasons for that. We have already looked at the concept of *fare bella figura* and, of course, *fare brutta figura*. In Italy we care a lot about appearances: it's to do with the sense of beauty and of 'what is right' for a particular moment and situation. This makes us especially susceptible to the way people look and behave superficially: so, for example, men with big cars and well tailored clothes are usually quite highly regarded in our society, regardless of the fact that they might just be crooks with a good sense of style.

Also, we place high importance on money: once nobility and important families were overtaken by merchants and bankers (a process that occurred in the Middle Ages and which brought many cities to a much higher level of importance in Europe), we learned that making your own success is more important than the name you carry. So, for example, in our modern culture, a celebrity or a rich person may hold higher status than a count or a princess just because he or she leads an intersting life, in the public eye, full of *'oggetti del desiderio'*, from diamonds to Maseratis.

And some of our titles, from *Commendatore* to *Cavaliere*, are mostly removed from any idea of family merit, and are given to people who have done special things with their lives.

I believe that the reason why, in the April 2008 elections, Berlusconi garnered a lot of votes might have a lot to do with this idea of money signifying prestige, but also with the idea that we have of the merits of climbing the social or professional ladder counting only on one's self. Berlusconi was a vacuum cleaner salesman who became Prime Minister. He has a degree, but much more importantly he possesses good business sense. He controls many of Italy's TV channels and part of the press. He was convicted of corruption and of many other offences arising out of his activity as an industrial tycoon (some members of his family were also convicted), but he still retained his position of prime minister, and in spite of his blackened record, people still actually listened to him. Even in our recent government crisis at the beginning of 2008, Berlusconi still seemed to have the nation's ear and was regarded highly, while Prodi, who indeed made many efforts to improve our country in many ways during his own time in government, and who is a man of values and culture, was somehow seen as a loser.

Is it because Berlusconi is more good looking (if you like that sort of thing)? Or is it because he is the symbol of a certain way of becoming successful? He certainly didn't cut a good figure after all the trials he had, but he is so good at the 'art of getting by' that he managed to stay afloat in every storm.

'His reputation as an entertainer who uses his media power politically is regarded by many Italians as a strength,' wrote Richard Owen in *The Times* (1 February 2008), 'He also has formidable personal charms and powers of persuasion ... There is a similar sneaking admiration for his defiance in the face of corruption charges, and many right wing voters agree with him that he is persecuted by left-wing magistrates...'. Owen also described Berlusconi as the 'Great Seducer', which is a nickname sometimes used for Silvio, it summarises quite well this image that we tend to have about him. Despite this, and the fact that he drew almost half of the votes in the April 2008 election, if you ask any voter in Italy, they will strongly deny having voted for him.

But Berlusconi can also be surprising: at the time of writing, he seems to have been able to build a government that is able to tackle tricky problems like rubbish collection in Naples and the question of the sale of Alitalia to foreign investors, and he's actually reducing taxes on property. The other novelty, it seems, is the shadow government built by Veltroni: for the first time Italy, like many other countries, has two big political powers instead of the old fractioning of powers between small political parties. This means that, for the first time, Italy's leaders might be better equipped to listen to everybody, the centre-right and the centre-left, and ultimately to deal with its problems in a more efficient way.

European papers have written that we don't have many women in politics in Italy. This is true, but things are improving. And those who are in power show a high quality of commitment. Some of them, from Letizia Moratti, minister of Education who led a big and important reform in our universities, to Emma Bonino, who speaks about feminism and women's rights, are well known abroad for their personalities and skills. But in the past some of our female members of parliament have appeared in the news because of a scandal or some particularly outrageous behaviour during a session in parliament or in a government crisis. It is true, though, that the current government seems to include some interesting women who are intelligent and hard working, although at time of writing it is still too early to talk about the performance of these politicians.

Certainly, a few years ago it was much more fun to watch the international news channels talk about Italy; it was the time of the aforementioned Ilona Staller and her Partito dell'Amore: she was against war, pollution, violence and fur. She also wore very little and used to be a porn star. The press were mad about her!

But people forget that our history hasn't been that simple. Women in politics are a relatively recent phenomenon, given that we were only granted the opportunity to vote in 1945. Before that, and sometimes even after that, women voting were considered – even by my own grandfather Remo – to be a potential disgrace. Wives belonged in the home, looking after children and their status wasn't very high, thanks in no small part to the church, which required women to be submissive for the good of society.

Women, in some cases, were also seen as somehow unstable, moody creatures: Italian men were wondering what these floaty beings would do once given the vote. Even when they did finally make it to the ballot boxes, many men went on believing that their place was in the house and keeping their hands out of politics was considered the best option.

So, when the 'sixties and the 'seventies arrived, and women became much more interested in politics, there still was a general tendency to prevent them from becoming important public figures: But things began to change very soon: there was among women a great admiration for Nilde Iotti when she became president of the Chamber of Parliament in the 'eighties, and later for Irene Pivetti, who in the 'nineties also attained this high position in our politics. But when the press mentions that numbers of women in Italian politics are still low, often those who write don't have a clue about our recent history and about the obstructionist tendency towards women by many male politicians in our country, which is now certainly diminishing, but which managed to stop us from accessing the highest places in politics as well as in other fields for many years.

Our constitution is also quite young: it was developed exactly sixty years ago, and 2008 is seeing all sorts of events marking the anniversary. A recent event at the Italian embassy in London was extremely interesting: among the people talking there was our ex-Prime Minister Giuliano Amato who spoke very extensively about the importance of the constitution and also about the contrasts that still exist in our country. He emphasised that the constitution was a huge achievement in 1948, and it came out of a country that was scarred by war but which wanted to look forward and give Italy a system of laws designed around the many needs and demands of the people. Our legal system is famously based, for the most part, on Roman law, where family had a capital importance, but many new aspects have been introduced in the past sixty years. The fact that celebratory events are taking place shows how much the Italians love, value and take pride in the constitution.

There's no denying that Italy has had a somewhat peculiar historical past, and geography, which makes us unique in many ways, for good or bad. Extensive problems like mafia, camorra, and recently illegal immigration, have plagued our country for many years, and we are still paying the price for brigandage – which, for some people, is at the origin of the Mafia in all its aspects and its perverse systems of reproducing and spreading. The well-known division between North and South has sometimes amplified the problems Italy has (as discussed in Chapter 1), and if you read the statistics on employment in Italy, it is very high in the North and still lower than average in the South. Our economy is also split into two: it's true, though, that in recent years the South has managed to count on some large companies employing new people, in sectors like furniture, electronics, cars and food production.

Also, what one could call a 'lack of legitimacy', as described by John Foot in his book *Modern Italy* is surely one of our worst problems: tax evasion, illegal construction and civil and political corruption have been constants in our history, and it's useless to deny this fact.

But the 'eighties marked a strong change in this trend. There have been large operations like *Mani Pulite*, (Clean Hands), led in the 'eighties and 'nineties by the magistrate Antonio di Pietro, which helped to collapse many illegalities and led to the conviction of corrupt politicians. *Tangentopoli* also unveiled a huge net of corruption in our politics, managing to fight against and flush out several dodgy members of our parties.

Anti-Mafia operations managed to shatter this establishment on several occasions, and many bosses and families have been handed over to the police. But it's not an easy fight: some magistrates who fought sharply against these crimes were killed in horrendous bomb attacks, like Giovanni Falcone and Paolo Borsellino; who died separately in 1992.

Our state is still suffering: it's a fact that even now this 'lack of legitimacy' is still our biggest problem: so, while we have beaten the political terrorism that plagued Italy in the 'seventies and 'eighties, Mafia and Camorra are often entwined with our politics, finance and economics, it has been this way for over a century; although things are slowly improving, some think that these entities will never really be completely beaten. In fact, some people believe that Italy will always be somehow stained by the 'criminal cartels', as they are called now: the vote of exchange, just to mention one huge problem in past years, was something that, especially, but not exclusively, in the South, contributed to political instability.

The idea of promising favours in exchange for the 'right vote' is something that has existed for a long time now, and, especially in places where getting a job is hard, it's easy to buy votes by promising a stable economic future to a family. It is unfortunately a sad reality that seems hard to change. In the April elections, though, some new rules were introduced to fight what was considered a potential problem: all mobile phones were taken from the voters, to avoid having people take pictures of ballot papers.

There is still a lot to be done about the question of the Mafia, in Italy and all over the world, as it's an international problem that interferes with business (including the fashion industry) and generally with life everywhere. Cooperation amongst the police, citizens, associations of all sorts and institutions has been bringing results, but there has also been a deep resistance against these people who want to change things.

The assassinations of important magistrates, but also of small politicians, mayors and even priests who have been wanting to change things, show that Mafia, Camorra and

Ndrangheta are active, alive and well, often very strong and still deeply involved with Italian and international politics.

* * *

It's necessary to accept the fact that there is still a lot of bad government in Italy. There is corruption at different levels, and several members of our parliament have been convicted of crimes. But the good side of our politics is often overlooked. At local level, and at regional level for example, I have direct experience of how hard our politicians work to make things better. I would say that our regions are shining examples of our best organisations in a political and social sense. We all feel we belong to our region more than to a common state: this is also because we can see that local governments usually work better, are more approachable and usually far removed from corruption and illegality.

Our regions receive subsidies from the state and invest greatly in education, transport, tourism, communications and the arts. We feel our taxes are too high generally, and this could have something to do with the fact that our top politicians and MPs are the best paid in Europe, enjoying the most privileges.

Major problems like brigandage in the late eighteen-hundreds were linked to discontent about taxation, and Italy has struggled to organise a modern tax-collecting system, which means we have people who simply don't pay taxes. Recently, Valentino Rossi and the actress Ornella Muti were targeted by the tax collectors and they are now paying huge amounts of money for the years in which they didn't pay adequately. I agree with Tom Foot when he writes that since 1945 taxes and tax evasion have been entwined with our poor opinion of the State. It's true that the system of taxation in our country isn't very efficient: there seem to be more taxes every year and many inequalities among the tax payers. Many of us feel this very strongly and it affects our vision of politics and generally of our state. We see politicians often as *'mangioni'* (heavy eaters or gluttons) and even thieves, and we have many expressions and proverbs that reflect this attitude. As a consequence, public people like the actor Beppe Grillo, whom I mentioned earlier, are more and more popular when they take action against a system that demands a lot but does not give much back to its citizens. The Italian people of course want stability and efficiency, homes, jobs, cheaper prices and fewer taxes. They don't want corrupt politicians. They don't want a state power consisting of tycoons and operators, mafiosi and camorristi. They want transparency and they want real people in the political sphere. Our young people especially believe something can still be done. In this hopefulness lies our future.

Thank God, we have some great people in politics too. There's Antonio Di Pietro, Francesco Rutelli, Emma Bonino; we have Walter Veltroni, and of course our president Napolitano. All these people, and more good politicians, are loved and highly respected, the young generations consider them symbols of integrity, and this improves the overall perception of Italian politics.

In a way, it also seems that our brand new government is gaining some respect from citizens, as it seems to want to improve things in Italy, but of course whether this will be successful will only be seen in the long run.

There's still hope, and we believe Italy is essentially a good country where things can work well when properly run, as they occasionally are. We have efficient public transport, good local administration, great schools, a good health system, positive signs in production and the economy, help for families and for those wishing to come and live in Italy. Also, for everything we hear about the Euro and the EU, Italy's adoption of the Euro currency actually brought with it *Tangentopoli* and the fight against corruption. During that time, a whole swathe of politicians were brought down, leaving room for respected financial leaders, Dini, Amato, Prodi and Ciampi, to carry Italy though the dawn of the Euro period.

In many ways, in fact, the Euro and EU presented many good opportunities for our country, and some of our trust in the state was restored. Of course people complained about the rise in prices and mourned the death of the beloved *lira*, but many of us understood that this step was a great thing for Italy.

We still, of course, like to blame the state for a lot of our problems – Italians tend to do this a lot: the State and politicians are what we love criticising the most. But we probably forget that a state is 'an autobiography of a nation', to quote what Gobetti wrote in the 'thirties, so we shouldn't really assume all fault lies with the state, but should also look at ourselves, at how we have been good at using the state's faults and failings, for example, at how we haven't reacted to corruption but instead have sometimes adapted to it. Illegality exists in many layers of our society, and corruption breeds corruption, as well as a tendency to distrust reforms.

We've had our fair share of political and economic highs and lows, and sometimes Italians wonder if this actually changes our lifestyle. But no other nation has been as good at remaining afloat when everything seems to be going bad. Each of us had to work a little bit harder but hasn't lost his or her smile. We are having children again, we keep producing Made in Italy products that sell, and we are positive, caring and warm and welcoming.

After all, even though it has been a long time since Byron was in Italy, and although the political situation is not at all the same, sometimes I think he captured the essence of our country very well in something he wrote to Thomas Moore in 1821: 'There is, in fact, no law or government at all [in Italy], and it's wonderful how well things go on without them.'

17. Italy and Religion: How Things Change

'The Vatican is a dagger in the heart of Italy'

– from Thomas Paine's Common Sense, 1776

THE FIRST TIME I SAW IT IT WAS A BIT OF A SHOCK: huge floats were coming towards me, richly decorated with flowers and golden fabric and carrying children in costumes, grow-ups with pretend beards, women with sky-blue cloaks holding crosses. On another float, a huge statue of the Madonna with a crown made of shiny stars was carried by four strong middle-aged men, and behind that another one with a statue of Saint Anthony carrying Jesus, another covered with flowers topped with a motionless female figure with long blonde hair wearing a purple and gold dress shining in the sun, surrounded by beautiful pink roses and lilies. Then the procession started: children dressed in the Azzurri football shirt carrying posters, and one by one, groups of women and men and young people all with different posters and flags.

Had I suddenly been transported to the south of Italy? Was it a dream? I had to ask a passerby: did they know what was going on? 'Oh, yes, it's only the Italian celebration of our Lady, it happens every year in Clerkenwell, it's all shut, you see, there's also a market where you can find Italian food, clothes…' And it was true: to the music of 1970s Italy, many stalls lined up in the sun were selling all sorts of things, from *torrone* to carnival masks, from home-made *ciabatta* to salami, Parma ham, just-made pizza and Italian football kits, all part of a huge festival of colours and flavours. On a corner, a little old man who apparently comes every year was selling small medals of Madonnas tied with green, white and red ribbons.

Seeing all that in the centre of London was incredible for me: it really was like going back decades in time and many miles south, specially because these things are not so common in Italy anymore. At an Italian Fair like this, with all its peculiarities and what we call *italianità*, you can basically relive an Italy that doesn't exist anymore.

Once, these religious processions, especially on Good Friday and other religious occasions, were at the heart of Italian life; it's still quite common to find them in tiny villages everywhere in the south, and in some villages in Tuscany, Marche, Umbria and Abruzzi. But in Italy it's now rare to see the faith that was animating the faces of those dressing up or holding crosses and statues; a procession like that in Italy would be something that's half-Carnival party, half village fête.

The latest decades have been crucial in this change. In the 1953 film *Pane, amore e fantasia* the village church is the centre of life for the tiny mountain place where the film is set. The women meet there to prepare the altar, to gossip about a forthcoming wedding or to actually pray. The social life revolves mainly around the eighteenth-century church where the priest often finds himself caught in the net of these gossiping ladies, and many funny situations ensue.

Often, fiction written in the post-war period and until the 'sixties regarded the church as the centre of social life: the young would meet in the church for catechism and the events in the religious calendar – from Lent to Pentecost, from Christmas to the Holy Assumption – would constitute important moments of the year. Fifty years later things have changed greatly. Religious practice is not the centre of our lives anymore, and the church is now mainly a place we go to for Christmas, Easter, first communions, weddings or funerals. Of course, some elements of this old tradition can still be found in Italy, again in the South for example, but also in rural areas all over Italy. Lively groups of youngsters still gravitate around the church in small villages, in schools we still teach the Holy Father prayer and celebrate Christmas with a nativity play. But churches are attended less and the Gospel and the Bible are no longer common reading books on our bedside tables. A multicultural society of course is only one reason for this change: when I was about twenty, at the end of the 'eighties, before there was mass immigration in Italy, we could already perceive how tradition was fading and how the habits of all of us were becoming influenced by a more secular view.

The pope, of course, remains the core of religion in Italy, and many thousands of people flood Saint Peter's Square every Sunday morning for the Angelus. The Church is and will always be an institution we respect, and religious values are still part of many people's lives. Church weddings and first communions are often big events: couples that get married with a civil rite are still very rare and often regarded as slightly abnormal. But with divorce now more common than twenty years ago and with the North becoming more and more similar to other northern European countries, the division between the 'two Italys' is becoming more distinct especially when we look at attitudes towards religion itself.

If you want to see a religious procession like the ones pictured in the film *Respiro*, where the Madonna is carried on a warm summer night along the streets of the village and then into the clear balmy waters of the Sicilian sea, you have to go south. There, in towns and villages, the Patron Saint is celebrated with a procession where the men carry the statue and the Holy relic and the women sing, the youngsters follow all dressed up in their Sunday clothes and generally the whole town takes part in the day. Events like the Fluidification of the Blood of San Gennaro are still called 'miracles' by our press. On 19 September, in fact, the miracle of making the blood melt and become fluid again inside its container is re-enacted, and people are intensely moved by this moment.

But if you see pictures of people witnessing miracles and of awe-struck Catholics at similar religious events, you are either in a Sicilian or Calabrian village … or in Clerkenwell, London. I think that our religious sense has somewhat evolved into a mixture of the sacred and the magical, and this mixture is evident in many ceremonies, like the Blessing of the Horse at the *Palio di Siena*, an essential part of the horse race. This rite is performed by the *Contrada* priest and contains elements of a sacred tradition and pagan principles to bring good luck to the horse.

Our attitudes to religion and morals are complex: we believe in our saints, we cry for San Pio di Terracina, but then we sanction abortion and the morning-after pill – the family is not as 'sacred' as it used to be.

Not many couples agree with the Pope's views on contraception – and in fact large families are becoming very rare in our country. I would say that our faith is evolving towards a personal idea of God. Ours is a religiosity which is more and more often entwined with a sense of help and charity. Not only in the name of religion only, but also in the name of altruism. Or in some cases because we particularly admire a religious leader: charisma is a strong thing.

One of my best friends, who is my age, is a priest. He's good-looking and charming, works hard at integrating more and more foreigners who come to his village and to the province where he lives, he promotes money collections and charity events for African projects and generally helps other people. He has also been to Kosovo several times to help there, despite having received threats by the local Mafia. He's a myth among his parishioners, as he often seems to forget about himself to help other people, to promote dialogue between different religions. The respect that he wins comes from Catholics, atheists, Muslims and Buddhists, and he's now setting up a community for people of all religious persuasions who want to pray and work.

People like him are rare: but they do keep our churches going. They get admiration and praise, especially because, in a lay society, where religion is becoming less of a priority and churches are closed every day because of a lack of priests, Italy still has some capacity for religion. The way people express their religious side has changed; fewer people pray, more people live in non-Catholic ways today. But the underlying principles of faith – generosity towards others, friendship and solidarity, charity and a good sense of togetherness that used to be the centre of religion – are still at the heart of our society.

Then, of course, there are the aesthetics of faith, the

visual aspect of our religion, so evident everywhere in Italy, and something Italians have always been attracted to.

The baroque churches in Sicily, with all their gold stucco and blue starry hearts, the beautiful Madonnas painted by the Medieval artists, the glory of our architecture are all symbols of our faith. Their attraction is still strong: religion is everywhere, sacred images are painted on the fifteenth-century walls in our towns, tiny churches are hidden in our countryside, and little *tabernacoli* with a Saint or Madonna are still everywhere. People put flowers in front of the sacred images and say a prayer when passing by. Some other people steal the Madonna statues and sell them to antiquarians ... but, as they would say, it's still a way to show appreciation!

When I was little I used to spend my summer holidays with my grandmother in Florence. My aunt, was the Mother Superior of a convent, so we would visit her and go to church quite a lot. This particular church had paintings and golden stuccos, framed pictures and gifts brought by people who had received miracles by the saints. All those shiny, beautiful, mysterious objects had a huge impact on me. Then of course there was all the charm and sexiness of the sacred paintings: Saint Sebastian I think was my favourite saint of all.

Being part of a family where the men have always belonged to the Socialist or Communist party and the women to the *Democrazia Cristiana* and were very close to the church, I grew up in a very unusual environment, where the men would swear for hours if hail had destroyed the wine grapes and the women would cover their ears and take the children away to protect them from all the drama and foul language.

But they all agreed on one thing: the same principles were all there, even if my grandfather was not religious and my father declared to believe in God but not in the priests or in the Pope. All my family agreed on matters like not having sex before marriage and not using contraceptives, but also on the importance of offering help to those that needed it, and being there to listen to a friend in need. Both the women and the men in our families were always available when there was the need to take somebody who could not drive to a hospital or to cook a meal for a neighbour who wasn't well. The idea of 'giving' has always been at the centre of our lives. The same goes for fidelity in marriages and being against abortion and divorce. In our family, which is huge, (I have eight aunts and uncles and forty-five first cousins plus a huge number of second cousins and great-aunts and -uncles), I have only ever heard of two divorces in our immediate family and one among my mother's cousins. The idea of staying together and actually dealing with problems together, even when the couple seems less strong, is something that our family has always believed in. This, and the idea of respect, comes from a strong religious background, but not exclusively: it's also from a long tradition of respect for the family itself.

The South has always had stronger religious traditions, and in my family's case, the fact of having many relatives in Campania has been crucial. On my father's side, my Southern grandparents were extremely religious just like the rest of the family. So, it was quite a contrast really: I was often quite struck by the different way religion was conceived, and still is, by the different sides of my family. But of one thing I am certain: the principles taught to us children by both sides of the family were inspired by the good, sound lifestyle that all of these people led. We are all very grateful for this.

On the other hand, as I mentioned, my Tuscan grand-father and great-grandfather had never set foot in a church apart from on their wedding days; at one point, when the Communists were considered enemies of the Church, Don Vittorio, the village priest in the late 'fifties, refused to bless our home because my grandfather was a Communist – something that always made me think of the stories by Giovanni Guareschi, that were translated into many languages. The idea of a small village in the 'fifties, and the feuds between two strong personalities, the left-wing mayor Beppone and the energetic priest Don Camillo, have always made me think of similar stories in lots of our villages not long ago, because these two sides of our history are still alive today.

With the *decreto* (decree) of 1989, *laicità* (secularity) is a 'supreme principle of the Italian Republic' so, although Vatican City is in Rome, in theory Italy is a lay state. But of course things can be different in reality: this is the nation where for months people have been hypnotised in front of the TV screen while the actor Roberto Benigni was reciting by heart several *Canti* of *The Divine Comedy*. Over eleven million people watched him at various times, and the actor himself, with all his declared left-wing tendencies, was so touched by the literary work and its meanings to actually give in to tears. Our nature is very intense and the spiritual side of things touches us sometimes very deeply. I have seen atheist cousins of mine become extremely moved when going to a church ceremony or to a cemetery.

However, we can't deny that Italy also has a long tradition of culture rooted in a lay background, and our ancient universities are very often linked to the secular tradition of learning and to the world of intellectuals who were part of centuries of scientific discoveries, from the age of Galileo and Leonardo.

Very recently there have been two events that are quite

symbolic, I think, in understanding the relationship between Italy and the Church (more than religion itself). A few months ago the Pope Benedict was invited to mark the start of the academic year at the Università la Sapienza, in Rome. But, despite the formal invitation sent to him by the rector of the University, not all of the professors seemed happy with the idea. So a scandal exploded when many of them wrote a letter saying that they didn't think the Pope would be the ideal figure to start the new year of learning, since, they added, he's often been opposed to science and progress! Of course there were strong reactions to these events: on one side, religious, traditionalist Italy was outraged by this, and the following Sunday there were about seventy thousand people in St Peter's Square to show the Pope their solidarity.

On the other hand, secular Italy did indeed hold the same view as the professors and students who found it inappropriate for a traditionalist pope to open the academic year in a progressive, modern university where science and research are so important. There were people who clearly remember the Pope's position on scientific giants like Galileo.

The second notable event was the row that exploded in the winter of 2007, when the Italian Synod of Bishops asked actors to refuse to take part in erotic scenes, after the release of the film *Caos Calmo*, by Antonello Grimaldi. The film starred acclaimed actor and director Nanni Moretti as a widower involved in an intense love story with a woman he saved from drowning. Some people described the comments of the bishops as out of place and talked about 'Vatican interference'. Even the celebrated film director Franco Zeffirelli, who is a committed Catholic, said that the Church is losing 'all sense of proportion'. So, again, the Church still holds a certain influence on our cultural expressions, and it is hard to imagine, in fact, Italy without this important aspect of our lives. It is also true that religion is becoming somewhat more strict after Pope Benedict arrived in the Vatican: there have been episodes of interference related to some types of art in churches, not considered to be 'in line' with the principles of faith, for example, something that people of all credos have opposed.

*   *   *

And then, of course, there is sex. Undeniably, there has always been a strong link, in our country and anywhere else in the world, between religion and sexuality.

Catholic morals have always been entwined with Italy and the Italians, for good or bad. But in our case this has somehow produced interesting mixtures in people's attitudes of the sacred and the profane.

For each of us, religiosity also means a deep link with passions and sex, love and sin. Although this seems like an old-fashioned concept, we all grew up in a Catholic environment (the large majority of Italians at least), so we feel quite strongly about this. Even if we don't go to church and we don't practice communion or confession, there will always be a little voice inside us wondering if what we are doing, desiring or thinking is 'good' or 'bad' in the eyes of God – something quite genuine and strong, really. But in Italy nothing is as simple as it looks.

One side of this is our preoccupation with physical appearance. Stephen Gundle has concluded that the Church, while offering models of motherhood and sainthood, hasn't been able to consistently change the importance that is given to beauty and external looks in Italy.

'Physical qualities are prized in the dominant culture and are culturally acknowledged. In this sense, the impact of the otherwise strong influence of Catholic culture in Italy encountered a limit. Catholicism reinforced the centrality of motherhood and the notion of a protective female function, while systematically downgrading female sexuality. However, the Catholic negation of the flesh, while it was very influential in the nineteenth century and for several decades in the twentieth, never suppressed or eliminated this substratum of popular culture. Nevertheless, Catholic efforts at repression shaped ideas of beauty and resulted in its being linked to approved female roles.'

Of course the Church has always had strong views on things like beauty contests, porn films and the image of women portrayed in advertising. But then there have also been contrasting views in the Christian Democratic party regarding these issues. Gundle quotes the words of Pia Colini Lombardi, a Christian Democratic member of parliament, who famously managed, in the 'fifties, to describe a connection between beauty contests and a 'higher' notion of beauty. 'Physical beauty publicises moral beauty … therefore more beautiful than all other women, and praised as such even higher than the stars themselves, is the Madonna'.

So, again, this relationship between image, sex, morals and the Church is quite unusual within the borders of Italy. And each of us has different opinions: when I asked some colleagues to describe the Italian man, one of them, Simonetta Losi, described a way of loving that 'has a pinch of sin inherited by Catholicism which is an added bonus'. Of course we are all conscious of this when we grow up: I had trouble overcoming these principles when I thought about sleeping with someone for the first time. We often have an ambivalent way of confronting this: something that other cultures consider extremely interesting. In fact, the idea of the 'Catholic woman' being divided between her principles and the idea of sin and redemption, and ultimately by the virginal idea of the woman on one side, and by the 'naughty' image on the other, are all deeply embedded in the idea of Italian and Mediterranean femininity.

Something I never really thought about until I fell in love with a foreigner: apparently, part of the reason why Italian women are so sexy in the eyes of foreign men is this image we offer of being divided between the Saint and the Sinner. Oscillating between the Madonna and the Whore, the Italian woman owes a lot to a Catholic culture that has shaped all of us. The Mamma and the Prostitute, the Wife and the Lover, the Friend and the Temptress, are maybe old stereotypes, but men love them.

And of course they have inspired endless literature, poetry and operatic works. So, aside from the values that the Church has somehow instilled in each of us, we should probably thank our religious country for everything it has done for our imagination.

18. 'Why We Chose To Live Like Italians': Interviewing the Italiani d'Adozione

'There is nowhere on Earth more naturally endearing than Italy...'

Richard Owen in The Times, December 2007

HOW MANY FOREIGNERS LIVE IN ITALY? AT THE beginning of 2007 they were three million, which is quite a lot considering that our economy hasn't been in brilliant shape during certain periods. But Italy has always been an attractive country for foreigners. As a holiday destination, of course, it stands among the most desirable in the world, but as a country to live in it has attracted huge numbers of people, from the Middle Ages right through to the present. As mentioned, there are dozens of books written in English about how to live and work in Italy. People from English-speaking parts of the world always seem to be have been very attracted to our country, and this doesn't seem likely to change.

It's interesting to notice that those journalists and writers who write dark, negative books or articles about Italy do actually live there. They are sometimes married to Italians, or they simply chose to take advantage of all that Italy has to offer: the sun, the food, the art, the beautiful people – yet still choose to write about our worst aspects sometimes. Just to quote one, Richard Owen has written many articles as the Rome correspondent of *The Times*, many of which are negative, but he does have to admit that 'nowhere on Earth is more naturally endearing than Italy...'. I think this is a perfect way to introduce this chapter.

So, why is it that in spite of bad press, more and more people choose Italy as a place to live? I am curious, slightly mischievous, and I am proud of being Italian. These three elements have pushed me to find out why, for example, so many people make Italy their home. I know quite a few: in fact, amazingly, among a total population count of less than one thousand people, the Vescovado di Murlo area has many English and American citizens who moved here quite a long time ago. And they keep coming! So what are the fascinating facts about our country that attracts foreigners, and also, what did the foreigners find difficult at first, and what advice would they give to those many more who are looking at Italy as a possible home?

I had a questionnaire handy, of course: nothing better than an interview to understand other people's views and dreams, and because I personally know most of these people, it was quite easy to talk to them and understand their ideas. It's always exciting to study the opinions of families who have emigrated.

I asked these people 4 questions:

1. When did you move to Italy and from where?
2. Did you know the country already? Had you been here before?
3. What would you say are the most attractive things in Italy for you? Some suggestions: the art, the climate, the food, the general beauty, the people, the history and culture, all of these, or other things?
4. How did you adapt at first? Did you find lots of differences between your own culture and that of Italy? How did you deal with them?

Simon Turner, a British translator who has been living in Italy for the past thirty years, finds that the main things he found attractive in Italy were all things I suggested, 'but also and possibly especially the fairly relaxed approach to life and the fact that, as a foreigner, I don't have to conform to the Italians' very conservative approach to fashion and other aspects of living.' Simon also adds that he has felt the influence of our lifestyle in different ways, but it was all positive: 'I have been influenced by the Italian dress sense and ideas about interior decoration, but I don't feel I have to follow all their strict codes and I'm not judged negatively if I don't.'

As for the process of adaptation, Simon didn't know the language, first of all, so this was a huge difficulty. He had been living in Florence for three months before moving to Turin and then Lucca, but living there permanently was different. 'Bureaucracy is bad in Italy, and it was much worse thirty years ago, but I soon learned that you can often get away with ignoring it entirely … Otherwise, I didn't find it hard to adjust – except that it was tough to find fresh cream, which became widely available only in the late 1980s or non-homogenised milk, which is still hard to find. Good apples don't exist here either, but really there's very little I miss and any disadvantages in the food world are more than compensated by all the rest Italy has to offer'. One thing that Simon doesn't find appealing about Italy is the television ... I wonder why!

I also got answers from an American woman who has been living in Italy for eighteen years. She came in the 'eighties from Newport Beach, in California to study in Siena and Florence. She finds that 'the country, people, food and climate' are the main reasons she finds Italy attractive, and she adds that after eighteen years she 'still finds the Tuscan countryside breathtaking. And the Italians are warm and social. When I first moved to Tuscany I was a vegetarian, that lasted for three months!'

As for differences, she describes mainly the day-to-day ones, like our lack of regard for queuing! 'At public places [banks, post offices etc] there are no lines, instead the Italians wait all together. So I would smile and be friendly!'

Monique Camarra moved from Canada to Italy in 1997 and she says she will never go back to Canada! 'I knew Italy very well and was very happy to move here as I had travelled to Italy at least once a year from the age of six months with my Italian parents.' She found it hard to adapt at first, as she found that there wasn't a lot of organisation about things, 'but then at one point I took off my watch, allowed myself to be 'late' for appointments ... went to have coffee with my students so I could enjoy the informal atmosphere that reigns here.'

The reasons why she loves Italy are all to do with the way of life we have there. 'The most attractive thing: freedom, having the sensation of being free ... Overall I would say there is a basic simplicity to living in Italy. Events are not manufactured, there are traditions that go so far back … For some reason things seem real here. In Toronto it seems that everything revolves around money, appearances. I am much more in touch with nature here. And the beauty is breathtaking: I always stop to admire it … Just sitting in the sun at my friend's *podere* is a moment of pure joy … Looking out onto the fields, rolling hills of grain, olive trees and the intensity of light and colour is peace … No one here makes an effort at 'manufacturing' this kind of atmosphere: it simply is like this'.

On the subject of people and relationships, Monique finds that everything seems more direct with the people in Italy. One strong example was when she fell pregnant just after having been hired for an important job teaching English in Italy. 'Relationships seem more human. When they called me to give me the definite offer I told them, thinking: OK, I've just lost this job. When I told my interviewer that I was pregnant, he stood up and gave me a huge warm hug saying that he was ecstatic about this news. Children are beautiful and the most important thing in life. I asked if this was going to have repercussions concerning my job. He looked at me and said 'absolutely not', and indeed it was that way. I had known this man all of three hours and that hug said a lot to me. I was in a human place. If my daughter was ever ill, it was expected that I drop everything and go home to be with my daughter; work could wait.'

As for friendship, Monique understood immediately how important it is for Italians.

'We don't have to organise well to meet up with people, because everything is so close and frankly, Italians put more emphasis and joy into meeting up with family and friends than getting the job done. When I say I can't come for dinner because I have to work on a project, I know deep down that

I can get organised enough to do my work *and* meet up with my family and friends here. That's the way it works. The people you know come first.'

Another aspect of life in Italy that Monique also noticed was the different kind of relationship we have with older people. As I said in the Family chapter, the older generations are respected and loved, and you don't just send somebody who is old to a home as they are an essential part of the family structure. 'I see the elderly and they are taken care of in the family. There's respect for all ages in life. You don't abandon them in some home or a hospital and you have real responsibility towards them. Sometimes you have to sacrifice, but that's life.'

As for the negative sides of life, Monique talked about two things that are quite interesting and that have a lot to do with our Catholic background. 'There seem to be two faces to life here. What you see on the surface and what everyone does privately. I think this stems from being in a Catholic country and in small cities where privacy is difficult to obtain. This said, human relationships are still important. Also it took me five years to get my drivers' licence because I was scared of driving amongst what I thought were crazy people on the roads. Now it isn't a problem … in total it took me three years to adapt to life here but now I wouldn't even think of going back to Toronto. This is my home'.

John is a 36-year old man who moved to Italy and decided it was his home, like Monique, but he had no connections to Italy apart from the image he had formed through the years. 'When I came here from Northern Indiana, USA, I had a small amount of knowledge based on Italian restaurants and coursework in school. Neither of these ways of learning about Italian culture really prepares one for the obsessive way in which Italians regard their food and their history, and it seems almost laughable until one allows him or herself to discover the beauty that can be experienced in a well-prepared meal or in visiting places that have catalyzed the growth of western culture for centuries'.

John finds that the attention to beauty is the most important cultural aspect of Italy and Italians: 'This perhaps comes from the richness of the natural and historical resources that surround them their whole lives. I think it's an excellent contrast to the attention to power and money that is prevalent in the US. Beauty is the central factor in the attention that Italians give to themselves, their clothes, their homes, their gardens, and their food – sometimes to a fault, but always with great style and a real love for the simple pleasures of life'.

John also adds that all the films you can see about Italy are not enough to actually give you an idea of how this country actually is. He found that this beauty is the first thing that made him fall in love with Italy, 'and the longer I stayed, the more layers of beauty I found in the ever changing rolling hills that are the luscious background to my daily walk to the grocery among the brick houses with their distinctive terracotta roofs.' This timeless beauty and the will to keep it protected from 'progress' also seems an important element for him: 'There is something about the architecture that makes one feel as if he or she lives in a timeless place that refuses the progress, pollution, and excesses of the rest of the modern world.'

Then of course, there is the people and their distinctive difference in culture compared to US populations. 'The people, as a general rule, are more passionate and display more emotion than Americans, making them generally seem more warm and friendly, but one learns to discover other layers of cultural barriers, insecurities and fears that are below the surface of this culture based on centuries of unspoken rules and superstitions.'

John really gets to the point in trying to unveil the mystery in our deep nature: and I found this fascinating as his point of view explains a lot of what the world sees in us.

'While some other expatriates I've met are turned off by the undercurrents of the Italian culture, I find them even more fascinating than the stereotypical passionate hospitality – even if I often run up against them in my ignorance. Trying to understand the motivations that drive Italian behaviour is like peeling the proverbial onion, and I find it to be a very attractive experience for one that decides to live in Italy for an extended period. For those who prefer people with simple, often boring personalities, where everyone is pretty much what he or she seems to be, the US is the right place.'

John didn't speak any Italian when he first arrived there. But he met his future wife, fell in love and decided to stay 'before I had learned enough Italian to carry on a meaningful conversation, speaking English with those who could and getting by on gestures and help from others who couldn't. Thus, the language was my first huge cultural issue that took essentially a year to resolve and another in which to become more or less comfortable.'

John also offers a very interesting perspective into the two different levels of Italian culture, on one side the global culture of Hollywood stars and reality shows, on the other side the local culture that carries on traditions at a neighbourhood level. 'There is an inherent pride in one's dialect, idioms, proverbs and regional identities – something that is less evident at a national level. Italy is like a lot of small culture centres that participate on an international level as a single nation, often with quite a bit of disagreement.' So when he started to go behind the apparent uniformity, he 'began to notice the differences between my own Midwest US culture and the infinitely more complex Italian culture'. Of course, he says he will never become Italian, although he can adapt to things on a superficial level. 'I had to adapt to the fact that there are no stores open twenty-four hours, that bars don't stay open until 3 a.m. that adults tend to live at home with their parents because they want to, that the salaries are excessively low for the cost of living, that certain parts of the year, streets are filled with tourists, that the streets are way too narrow, that nepotism is an accepted rule, and that for what a small apartment costs in Italy, in many places in the US you can buy a large house with a swimming pool.'

But John decided that, for all these differences, he wanted to stay in Italy, and he accepted these differences as conditions of living in this country, and obtaining the benefits that come with living there. 'In many ways the things to which I had to adapt can be considered to have had positive effects on my lifestyle, and I am happy with my life in Italy'.

Sarah Wadsworth, an Englishwoman, first moved to Italy in 1970, she lived in Milan with her ex-husband for a time where she wondered if that was what she actually wanted. She didn't know the language and she found that 'everybody seemed very involved in politics and women in trying to lead a man's life.'

Society was very different during that period, and adapting was hard. 'At the time, I was plunged into bourgeois Milanese society in the early 'seventies where live-in maids were normal. I would meet my contemporaries buying their bread in the morning dolled-up in their minks, with me in my jeans and desert boots … It took another ten years or so for them to catch up on some of the Anglo-Saxon ways of living.'

Sarah has now spent a total of thirty-five years living in Italy, and she says that in spite of the drawbacks, she 'wouldn't swap it for anywhere else'. What does she like about Italian lifestyle so much? 'The way of life, the people and the climate are obviously interconnected and consequential: the innate generosity and affection, hospitality and desire to please make life so much easier and pleasanter. The history and culture are part of your surroundings, although our modern era doesn't seem to be able to produce anything very great on Italian home ground. Then of course there's the food and drink. Where else can you personalise your order in a restaurant: with or without garlic, more or less basil, no tomato in the sauce, *un pizzico di questo, quello* (a pinch of this and that) ...'

What about the drawbacks Sarah mentioned? 'Conservatism abounds, change is not often welcome. Discovering with time that the schools and hospitals were completely dominated by political hierarchy was very difficult for me to accept, and right through my children's schooling, I always got myself voted class representative in an effort to understand how it all worked'.

So, it is evident that, although there often is, obviously, a lot of adjusting to do for somebody who comes from a different culture and lifestyle, all these people have decided that the good sides beat the bad sides by miles. That is why they stay in our country and the idea of going back doesn't really cross their minds. The endearing side of Italy, with all its richness and history and beauty, the warmth of its people and climate, represent something you won't give up even if sometimes there might be confusion in politics or a bit too much bureaucracy...

In fact, just like Julie Donald, a Scottish woman who has been living in Italy for a long time after travelling for years, underlines, there are many attractive things besides the beauty, the food and the nice people. It's an ideal country in which to bring up children. 'The quality of life in terms of safety, a life that is less frenetic, where it's good to bring up children because of the family values that are here and the sense of community you can feel in small villages like ours, are all things we love. We first moved to Molise in 1991, and for me it was difficult, as I didn't understand the dialect. But my experience in Japan had taught me that it's possible to live in a country and get to know the people and culture slowly before actually speaking the language. It was challenging, of course. But here, in Italy, I love the diversity of the regions, I sometimes feel there is no need to travel outside Italy because each region is so diverse and full of interesting things to see and do.'

Is there anything she would never give up? 'Yes, many things. The food, and the family sitting around the table together, is a wonderful moment. And then there is the *passeggiata*, to go slowly up and down the main street of Siena, the *corso*, in your best clothes on a Sunday afternoon.'

And Finally - Italians Do ... and Italians Don't ... : Some Tips on How to Live Like an Italian

Italians DO eat a lot of pasta: Italians DON'T flood their pasta with cream and cheddar cheese

IN LONDON I PUT ON ABOUT TEN KILOS AFTER THE birth of my second child, thanks to all the fried food and snacks you find everywhere. But I lost it all again in 2004 and never put it back on, thanks to Mediterranean food and Weight Watchers. There they confirmed that pasta is really good for you when you try to lose weight, as it doesn't contain fats and it keeps you full and satisfied for longer. When I go back to the meetings to check my weight, I sing the praises of pasta: what's funny is that sometimes I've had people say to me: 'Oh yes, I love pasta, especially with lots of Cheddar cheese on top.'! Cheddar on pasta is not slimming! Try a

213

teaspoon of Parmesan cheese and a teaspoon of olive oil: then you can eat happily and be sure not to put weight on. The fat we put *on* the pasta is what makes us fat: not the spaghetti!

Italians DO love pasta: real Italian pasta doesn't come in a can!

Yes, believe it or not, pasta rings, pasta letters, and canned spaghetti with meatballs ARE NOT Italian dishes. We don't have canned ravioli in Italy either, and we don't know what pasta rings are, thank God.

Italians DO love their wine – Italians DON'T drink themselves silly

In Italian the expression 'hangover' doesn't exist, which says a lot about us, really.

We produce some of the best wine in the world but, as I said in the food chapter, the drinking culture is so very different in Italy: wine is not seen as something to forbid, so our teenagers are not eager to transgress the law on age limits because *we don't have one*. Ten-year-olds are given small samples of wine to try with their steak: so wine is not seen as forbidden. We don't find that getting drunk helps the fun, and, while in Trafalgar Square on Saturday night you can see few people walking straight, going to an Italian party will teach plenty of people that there is a lot of fun to be had when your head is clear … and plenty more sociable moments to enjoy when you can actually *remember* what you did and said the night before.

Which is why…

Italians DO love partying – Italians DON'T need extra help to do it

What is less attractive than alcoholic breath straight in your face when you are at a party or in a bar? We Italians believe that being drunk is the opposite of being sexy. Of course we like our champagne and wines, but in moderation, and when we want to meet somebody, starting to talk to them is not hard for us, even if we didn't touch a drop of alcohol. Most of the time, we have the 'courage' to talk to new people without having to find strength in a glass of something alcoholic.

My husband thinks it's a matter of cultural characteristics: while in Italy people smile at you even if they don't know you, and they socialise very spontaneously, make eye contact and hold it with no trouble at all, centuries of repressive education has influenced countries like Britain and here things like that don't come as naturally. But there is another reason why our parties are so different from British ones: *we serve food with the alcoholic drinks*!

The pub culture: going for one, two, six pints to be had with peanuts or crisps, is influencing the way people think of parties as well. In my case, I couldn't imagine a party without food, and when I moved to London I was quite shocked to discover that at most of the gatherings in the UK you will be served 'drinks and nibbles'. Nibbles? That's what we call Stuzzichini, but since they are meant to *'stuzzicare l'appetito'* (stimulate your appetite), we serve them before the real food, which is always there at a party! That's another reason why we don't get as drunk, since drinking on an empty stomach is very different than drinking while 'nibbling' on a plate of meat crostini, sliced ham, bruschetta and roasted vegetables.

Italians DO love their cars: Italians DON'T believe in driving safely

I will have to agree with the stereotypes on this one. Some of our towns are the most chaotic in Europe. We are notorious for not stopping at traffic lights and for too many accidents during the weekend. As Beppe Severgnini wrote, we see traffic lights as a challenge, not as a reason to stop. But things are changing: the relatively new system of points to be marked on the driving licence for driving offences is really working, and people pay much more attention now to speed limits and to parking restrictions, as nobody wants to lose their driving licence for something they could easily avoid.

Italians DO have to deal with bureaucracy: Italians DON'T queue up to do it

When I interviewed people who moved to Italy from the US and other English-speaking countries, one pattern emerged: the lack of queues in Italy has left many of them perplexed. Of course, for a country like England, where you still have to queue to get on a bus, Italy must seem a ruthless place. When I moved to the UK, and I tried to get on a bus, a lady looked at me and, red in the face, said: 'In THIS country we queue up, you know…'

So, maybe because of complaints by foreigners, or to speed up the office work, in recent years a system of numbers has been introduced, so at the entrance of public offices there is now a small machine that issues numbered tickets, and then each person gets called in an orderly fashion … almost like in civilised countries, really!

Italians DO come from the South of Europe:
Italians DON'T look much like their neighbours ·

What do we have in common with the Spanish, French, Greeks, Turkish, North Africans? A certain look maybe, the warmth of our behaviour, our love of good things like parties and food, and music and love.

But Italians do look and feel different from their Mediterranean cousins almost as much as from their English-speaking friends. Somehow, we feel unique, and of course, if sometimes people generalise, we are individuals and it's hard to *'fare di tutta l'erba un fascio'* (tie all the grass in one single bunch), as we say.

So Italy is unique, the Italians are unique, the Tuscans and the Neapolitans are unique, and each single one of them is different from the rest. But if you can recognise an Italian family among hundreds of them visiting Trafalgar square just by the way they walk, then there must be something typical of our Nation.

Of course, the exoticism of the Italians is not just a stereotype: we have attractive national characteristics. In books and films such as A *Room with a View*, the British holidaying in Italy not only marvel at the stupendous Tuscan scenery, but also at the difference between the Italians and the British people. The different approach to life is celebrated in these works: this difference is part of the appeal that the British find in a town like Florence. And ultimately, it might be part of the reason why so many foreigners have found so much romance and poetry in us as a population.

Our warmth and accessibility to others is hopefully something that will never change; Byron, Shelley and Joyce loved it as much as modern travellers do. If we want to make friends, we don't need alcohol or drugs to help us break the ice: just a smile. Italy's beautifully multicultural society is having numerous effects on our lives in Europe and it will be more and more difficult to generalise, to enclose one nation in a series of definitions. Perhaps generalising is always a bad thing, as many argue. Each individual person is different, and so the idea of sharing 'national characteristics' may be outdated and overly simplistic. But, like many other people, Italians still love to think that they can 'feel' and recognise each other at any latitude. It has happened to me many times, realising that I was looking at Italians before I could actually have proof of it. We like to believe in 'Italianità', and to think that fundamentally, the Italian nature is deeply different and unique. Taking this idea of Italy abroad, mixing with all sorts of people and cultures yet keeping our individuality has always been important to us: maybe this attitude is the key to our intense but harmonious relationship with the rest of the world.

Appendix: The Italian Directory

HOW DO YOU CHOOSE THE BEST PLACES TO BUY FOOD, wine, fashion, cars, properties, ceramics, wines and jewellery from Italy? How do you pick the best Italian restaurants? London and the UK are full of places like these, and though I may not necessarily be able to name the definitive Italian delicatessen in London or the best bar, I can rely on my own personal taste and 'insider knowledge', on my friends who like Italy, and on the websites I write for. What you will find here is a small but objective selection of good places and websites where it's easy to find good Italian stuff. Then you can judge for yourself. I will also give a handy list of Italian events that happen in the UK. I will divide this part according to the order of the chapters of the second part of the book.

First, just a few names of fairs, events or places connected to Italy to be found in the UK: the most famous is probably *La Dolce Vita* at Olympia in London, which takes place every year in March (second weekend): www.ladolcevitaevent.co.uk.

The Italian Film festival has become an important event both for England and Scotland: check the dates and locations at www.italianfilmfestival.org.uk.

At the Riverside Studios in London they run Italian theatre seasons and connected events, interviews with actors and film makers, etc: www.riversidestudios.co.uk.

At the Italian Bookshop in Cecil Court, WC2, you can find Italian books, DVDs and music, but you can also meet new and famous writers who meet there to present their latest work (I launched my Italian book there in London in November 2006). It's also a favourite for people who want to discuss politics, and the right place to meet celebrities … Ornella Tarantola and her colleagues will welcome you with their typical Italian smiles…www.italianbookshop.co.uk.

For those Catholics (or anyone else) who want to experience Italian spirituality but also for those who just want to be in touch with Italian events like carnivals, parties, dinners and dances, charity events, fairs, or just have an Italian espresso the way it should be, St. Peter's Italian Church in Clerkenwell is the ideal place. There are also Italian courses for children run by the Italian State and youth clubs every week, a range of activities like youth games and parties of all kinds: www.italianchurch.org.uk.

For information on anything regarding Italian travel, visas, bureaucratic matters, etc, visit www.it-consul.org.uk, the site of the Italian consulate, and www.amblondra.esteri.it. For great music, art and design events, culture (conferences by writers and poets, piano and literary competitions, exhibitions of photography and painting), Italian classes and so on, visit the site of the Italian Cultural Institute in Belgrave Square, WC1, – and the ICI itself, with its stuccoes and magical atmosphere: www.italcultur.org.uk.

Escape in Art is an association promoting Italian culture and theatre in the UK. They also organise literary competitions and literary events all through the year: www.escapeinart.com.

There are other associations and art clubs in London: I contribute to some of the sites myself, including www.giorgiostudio.co.uk and www.italiansoflondon.com.

Many magazines online deal with Italian food and art, including *Italia!* magazine, www.italia-magazine.com, *Italuita online* magazine, www.italvita.co.uk, a guide to all things Italian, and *Italy* magazine, www.italymag.co.uk.

FOOD AND DRINK

Here are the five main delicatessens that I love in London (some don't have websites).

Carluccio's South Kensington and other London locations
Lovely atmosphere, modern environment, and tables to eat or have cappuccino or coffee in a designer café that offers many specialities from pasta to olive oil. Not cheap. www.carluccio.co.uk

Delizie d'Italia 70 Lupus Street Pimlico SW1
Marcello and his friends, all from the warm South of Italy, assure a warm welcome, beautiful home-made dishes and hot drinks, a small series of outdoor tables to have a quick ciabatta or a good dense Italian-style hot chocolate. Good for bread, also Tuscan, baked every day, and pastries. Not cheap either but worth the money.

Olga 30 Penton Street Islington N1.
I used to live round the corner from Olga's: she is an

institution not just for Islington. Her salami, olives, cheese and general groceries are beautiful. No space really for sitting down and having your lunch, but brilliant for choice.

Gazzano's Farringdon Road, Clerkenwell
Brilliant for cheap and fresh food, long-life packed pasta and cakes, and for a huge selection of affordable specialities from all over Italy. Not to be missed.
www.tipped.co.uk/listings/58060/Gazzano's

The Rosslyn Rosslyn Hill, Highgate
An upmarket selection of food and drinks from France, Italy and other Mediterranean countries. Very nice shop with plenty of choice, but it's the most expensive of the five. Worth it, though. www.delirosslyn.co.uk

* * *

There are many companies that offer Italian food delivered to your door and in some cases also catering for parties, etc. The best I have used are:

Natoora (ex-Portobello Food company) which offers a good range of Italian and French food, but also Italian cleaning products, cosmetics, fruit and vegetables ready for use (for minestrone, risotto, etc.) www.natoora.co.uk.

The other website, something of a competitor to Natoora, is www.nifeislife.com. I personally use both, as sometimes one may not have the thing I need.

Another wonderful site to visit for Italian catering and for Italian cookery lessons in your home, www.invitemetodinner.co.uk. Giovanna Plebani and Co. can also prepare wonderful food for you for events and special dinners.

Wines

How to shop for good Italian wines? At present, most supermarkets stock good Italian wines, so we often don't feel the need to look for wines anywhere else.

If you are looking for something really different though, that you might not find in supermarkets or high-street wine retailers, then visit these websites: www.italianwines.com, www.wineshop.it.

Restaurants and cafes

After the disappearance of Pollo, the wonderful *trattoria* in the West End with red and white checked tablecloths and wonderful pasta dishes for a fiver, London is left with many Italian restaurants but very few with that real Italian feel to them. One not to miss is of course the iconic **Bar Italia,** a twenty-four hour café where in fact the atmosphere is possibly better than the food, which tends to be expensive and not exceptional. The photos of the 2006 World Cup victory celebrations at Bar Italia have gone around the world thousands of times! Interesting fact: in 1926, John Logie Baird first demonstrated television in a flat over the Café Italia, apparently! www.baritaliasoho.co.uk

A bar not to be missed in Covent Garden is the glorious **Frank's Café** at 52 Neal Street, established in 1922 and now an institution. At the Café, only open until 8pm and not on Sundays, Salvatore and Trofimena from Minori on the Amalfi coast prepare amazing Italian dishes like risotto and ravioli as well as traditional fry-ups for a breakfast to be remembered.

Another Bar, which is also a renowned restaurant, is in Marylebone: **Caffè Caldesi**, and it's owned by the Tuscan

Giancarlo Caldesi, a BBC cook who also runs a cookery school (www.lacucina.caldesi.com) and also has a restaurant outside London, www.campagna.caldesi.com.

In the Holborn area, **Lo Sfizio** offers pasta dishes and snacks of good quality, (35-37 Theobald's Road) www.sfiziocaffe.com

Belgravia seems to be the area to go if you prefer beautiful (but not cheap) Italian cookery in a classy atmosphere. The best Italian restaurants are indeed in this area, and they offer simple dishes with great ingredients. **Oliveto**, at 49 Elizabeth Street SW1, offers simple, amazing dishes (my friend Fabiana once saw Woody Allen eating there!). www.restaurant-guide.com/oliveto.htm

Olivo Mare, at 10-12 Lower Belgrave Road, SW1, also has a beautiful reputation for food, wines and atmosphere. It serves excellent fish dishes.

Il Convivio, 143 Ebury Street, SW1 is a Tuscan restaurant in the same area, again an amazing place for Tuscan recipes, but also simple and amazing dishes. www.etruscagroup.co.uk/ilconvivio.htm

Osteria dell'Arancio at 383 Kings Road, SW10. Great food but especially great wines. www.osteriadellarancio.co.uk

My personal favourite, **The Italian Kitchen,** at 43 New Oxford Street, where I went with my husband the night we got married (the *first* time we got married!).

Their desserts are fantastic, which, for somebody who eats only the best desserts, is a serious endorsement, www.italiankitchen.uk.com.

And where do you go to find real Italian ice cream? There is only one place: **Oddono's** in Kensington, 14 Bute Street, SW7 3EX. Oddono's was a finalist at the Retailer of the Year Award 2007 and offers an incredibly delicious range of flavours, all made with fresh ingredients and created rigorously by hand. www.oddonos.com

And if you want to buy real extra virgin olive oil straight from the Tuscan producers, where do you go? Try our farm, belonging to my mother's family Carapelli (not related to the Carapelli olive oil makers of Florence) since the 1920s. We make the real thing: cold-pressed extra-virgin olive oil from our two hundred olive trees, in fields that overlook Lupompesi and the surrounding areas with breathtaking views.

Our oil is produced with certified methods that conform to the regulations of the *Consorzio dell'Olio Toscano* (www.oliotoscanoigp.it) which include the best olive oil producer of Tuscany and gives the IGP (*indicazione geografica protetta*) only to the best ones. We got it! So just write to: anl.c@hotmail.co.uk for more information.

* * *

MORE ITALIAN SERVICES, PLEASE...

On many occasions, like weddings and First communions, wedding anniversaries and even graduations, the Italians have a passion for giving something we call *bomboniere*, a small gift to take home which contains the names of the people who got married or took a degree, a small gift and some sugared almonds, called *confetti* in Italian (nothing to do with the usual wedding confetti, which we call *coriandioli*, which we also throw at carnivals). Because of the high numbers of ceremonies connected with the Italians living all over the world, some clever Italians have started to produce these *bomboniere*, but they are still not so easy to find. For my boys' First Communions I was advised to go to this fantastic site: www.bombonieremania.co.uk, run by Luisa Morena. A must for those who want to celebrate the Italian way. What about Italian cakes for ceremonies or special occasions? Bomboniere Mania also provide cakes for ceremonies.

Photos for your parties or celebrations? You need Giorgio di Marzo at GiorgioStudio, www.giorgiostudio.co.uk. As for Italian hairdressers, there are a few I could recommend, but my favourite is darling Yuri Ghiori from Arezzo, who will come to your house and do wonderful things with your hair without you having to walk out of the door.

There's plenty more to say about Italian services of course: Italians are all over the world and everywhere they go they have managed to bring that special touch of class and taste when it comes to food, wine, beauty, parties, special treats, etc. But this is not a guide to services, it's a guide to how to live like an Italian, wherever you are in the world – and if you have read up to here, you must know by now how to do it almost as well as Italians themselves! So just follow my advice: relax and let the Italian inside you take you on a sensuous tour of flavours and colours.

Acknowledgements: Grazie A ...

FIRST OF ALL, THANK YOU TO MY AGENT, Lorella Belli of LBLA, for seizing the opportunity presented to her by Anova Books to find an Italian author for this book. She thought of me straightaway, and her trust is something that still moves me.

Thanks to my editor, Barbara Phelan, who has put up with me and with my unusual way of expressing myself in a language that isn't mine. It's one thing speaking English every day, having studied it for years before moving to the UK, and quite another to write sixty-five-thousand words on topics that are not always easy.

Thank you to the following people who have replied to various questions and have offered various assistance through email, and personally, about topics like the image of Italians abroad, Italian men, how things have changed in the field of love and relationships, the Italian outlook on families, how it has been to move to Italy from another country and so on. *Grazie a*: Nico Tulini, Simonetta Losi, Andrea Semplici, Michèle Flavio Borgogni, Susanna Vimercati, Giancarlo Pepe, Don Domenico Poeta, Umberto Genovese, Elisa B, Harriet Nowell-Smith, Marta Lusini, Tim Nowell-Smith, Cornelia

Pfeffer, Giorgia Scaturro, Antonio Vigni, Jevon Brunk, Simone Berni, Clover Southwell Duccio I, Giovanna Plebani, Roberto F, Andrea Bechi, Jerry and Toby Levine, Maria Elena Tondi, Mauro Limiti, Francesco, Nicola Ulivieri, Sarah Wadsworth, Monique Camarra, Vanessa Santoni, Simon Turner, Nicoletta Sinatti, Angela Young, Fabiana Dalpiaz, Massimo Sollazzini, Julie Donald, Juri Ghiori, Benedetta Sgroi, *zia* Giulia Zamperini, Angela Lobina, Emanuele Lobina, Lorenzo Lanini, Marta Santamaria I Llavall, Michelle, Gabriele Fanetti, Giorgio di Marzo and Paolo Minoli.

A special thanks to my family: Rob, Francesco, Joe and my mother Tosca were all very supportive and also gave me interesting comments and suggestions, starting with my son Joe helping me with the Sports and with the Music chapters, my husband giving me help with developing ideas and suggestions on what he loves about Italy, and Francesco being imaginative and helpful with the sunny image he has of Italy. Rob also provided comments on Italy from his own perspective that were very important, and my mother gave me recipes and advice for the food chapter. Thank you to my brother-in-law Dick Nowell, who has supported me in my literary enterprises since I moved to the UK.

I am also grateful to Stefania Bochiccio from the Italian Cultural Institute in London who has been sending useful material and invitations, and to Roberto Orlando, press officer of the Italian Embassy, for the same reason. Last but not least, *grazie* to Beppe Severgnini, Daniel Franklin and John Lloyd who took part in a wonderful event about Severgnini's book *La Bella Figura*, in 2007 at the Italian Cultural Institute. Their conversation was extremely useful to me – and very entertaining.

Finally, I must thank Professor Stephen Gundle for very kindly providing the foreword for this book.

Bibliography and Sources

ALL QUOTATIONS IN THE BOOK ARE REPRODUCED by kind permission of the author and/or publisher.

Beppe Severgnini, *La Bella Figura: A Field Guide to the Italian Mind*, Hodder & Stoughton, 2006

Russel Ash, *The Top 10 of Everything 2007*, Hamlyn, 2006

Stella Donati, *Cucina Regionale Italiana*, Euroclub Italia, 1992

Tutto Ferrari, Mondadori, 1997

www.repubblicasalentina.it

Martin Solly, *Xenophobe's® Guide to the Italians*, Oval Books, 2007

Elizabeth David, *Italian Food*, Penguin 1977

Lucia Lazari, *Cucina Salentina*, Mario Congedo Editore

John Foot, *Modern Italy*, Palgrave Macmillian, 2003

Grazia Piccardi, *'Coppie, il Boom dell'Italia mista – Uno su sette con partner straniero'*, article published in *Il Corriere della Sera*, 30 January 2008

Richard Owen, 'Silvio Berlusconi "The Great Seducer" Set to Charm His Way Back into Heart of Power" ', article in *The Times*, 1 February 2008

Richard Owen, 'The Italian Slob – A Nation That Defined the Good Life Must Relearn How to Live It', article in *The Times*, 22 December 2007

'*Immigrazione, circa 3 milioni di stranieri residenti in italia al 1 gennaio 2007*' article from *Agenzia Quotidiana di Stampa I Fatti*, 2 October 2007

www.maserati.com

www.ferrariworld.com

www.colani.ch (Luigi Colani's site)

www.murlocultura.com

www.comune.murlo.siena.it

Programme of *Festa Medievale Murlo* 2000, *Associazione Sportiva Dilettantistica Vescovado*

Jeremy Clarkson, *I Know You Got Soul*, Michael Joseph, 2004

www.italtrade.com

www.italiamia.com

Sofia Gnoli, *Un secolo di moda italiana*, Molteni, 2006

'The History of Italian Cinema', Wikipedia

T. Neighbour Ward and Monica Larner, *Living, Studying and Working in Italy*, Owl Books, 2003

Claudia Roden, *The Food of Italy*, Vintage, 1999

Adrian Michaels, 'Naked Ambition', article in *The Financial Times*, 13 July 2007

http://ospiti.comune.siena.it/filoerba/aeroporto/herald.html

Nancy Harmon Jenkins, *The Flavours of Tuscany*, Broadway Books, 1998

Casilda Grigg , 'An Amorous Offer You Can't Refuse', article in the *Independent*, 3 December 2007

Casilda Grigg, 'Marco's Top Ten Flirting Tips', article in the *Independent*, 3 December 2007

Richard Owen, 'Mamma's Boys', article in *The Times*, 8 January 2008

www.ludovicoeinaudi.com

www.italtrade.com (Musikmesse – The Italian Sound will delight the world's ears)

'Brothers in Harmony', article in Relative Values, the *Guardian* magazine, December 2007

www.unicef.it

www.gss_svizzera.ch

Rossella Cadeo, '*Qualità della vita, vince Trento*', article in *Il Sole 24 ore*, 17 December 2007

Ian Fisher, 'In a Funk, Italy Sings an Aria of Disappointment', article in *The New York Times*, 13 December 2007

Ian Fisher and Elisabetta Povoledo, 'Italy Struggles under Truck Strike', article in *The New York Times*, 13 December 2007

Ian Fisher, 'Defying Critics, Italy's Leader endures', article in *The New York Times*, 6 December 2007

'Non sono giovane', Igiaba Scego, article in N*igrizia*, December 2007 (www.nigrizia.it)

Pellegrino Artusi, *Il nuovo Artusi. L'arte di mangiar bene*, Mursia, 2007

www.invitemetodinner.co.uk

www.canali.libero.it

www.vespa.com

www.gilera.com

www.piaggio.com

John Foot, *Calcio: A History of Italian Football*, 4th Estate, 2007

Stephen Gundle, *Bellissima: Feminine Beauty and the Idea of Italy*, Yale University Press, 2007

Robert Lumley, Paul Ginsborg and John Foot, *Italian Cityscapes: Culture and Urban Change in Contemporary Italy*, University of Exeter Press 2004

Thomas Glyn Watkin, *The Italian Legal Tradition*, Dartmouth 1997

John Foot, *Moggiopoli*, LR Books, 2006

Paul Ginsborg, *A History of Contemporary Italy: Society and Politics 1943–1988*, Palgrave MacMillian, 2003

Giovanni Guareschi, *The Little world of Don Camillo*, The Reprint Society, 1953

www.aboutitaliandesign.info

www.italiamia.com

www.italophiles.com

www.italymag.co.uk

www.dolcevita.com

www.cucinait.com

www.winesoftuscany.com

www.virtualitalia.com

www.ciaoitaly.com

www.filastrocche.it

www.exhibart.com

www.museionline.com

Guido Santevecchi, 'Living La Dolce Vita', article in the *Guardian*, 4 July 2006

John Hooper, 'Organised Crime Does Pay in Italy, To the Tune Of €90 bn', article in the Guardian, 24 October 2007

'Quality Food "In Great Health" ', article in *Italy* magazine, 19 November 2007

Flavia Laviosa, 'The Post Modern Italian Family, Or The Reality Changes But the Word Stays the Same", article in Humanising Language Teaching Online Magazine (www.hltmag.co.uk)

Giovanna Casadio, '*Oggi il family day in pizza. Napolitano: non discriminare I gay*', article in *La Repubblica* 12 May 2007

Alessandro Rimassa, '*Trentenni/lavoro casa e famiglia dopo I 30*', article in *Affari Italiani*, online daily (su canali.libero.it)

Richard Brooks and John Follain, 'Forget 4-4-2 Lads, Let's

Talk Kandinsky', article in *The Sunday Times* 16 December 2007

Hugh McIlvanney, 'Capello Ruthless and Right', article in *The Sunday Times*, 16 December 2007

Ian Hawkey, 'Don't Fool with Fabio', article in *The Sunday Times*, 16 December 07

Gianmaria Padovani e Lucia Scajola, '*Italiane da Export/Fabriquée en Italie*', article in *Panorama*, 3 January 2008

Andrea Semplici, (translated by A. Coppolaro-Nowell), *Asmara*, in *The Architectural Review*, October 1999

David Raizman, *History of Modern Design*, Laurence King Publishing, 2003

Bill Risebero, *The Story of Western Architecture*, Herbert Press, 2001

500-Il ritorno di un mito, editrice la Stampa spa, 2007

Rainer W. Schlegelmilch, *Formula 1: 1950 – Today*, Feierabend Verlag, 2004

The Oxford Companion to Music, Oxford University Press, 1956

Cecilia Bolognesi, *Design City Milan*, Wiley, 2007

Geoffrey Nowell-Smith, *The Oxford History of World Cinema*, Oxford University Press, 1997.

The Fashion Book, Phaidon, 1998.

Art Deco, 1910–1939 (edited by E Benton, T Benton, G Wood), V&A Publications, 2003.